I0606377

by
Justin Melo

Minneapolis, Minnesota

DEDICATION

This book is dedicated, with gratitude, to the following people: To my partner, Anna, for believing in me and always encouraging me to chase my dreams; to my parents, for giving me the best example of what parenthood is supposed to look like; to my older brothers Gary and Jessie, for fueling my love of sports; to my sisters-in-law Nancy and Stephanie, for being the sisters I never had; to my wonderful nieces and nephews Max, Leila, Zac, Zoe, and Myla, for adding a new layer of happiness to my life; to the Corbo family, for making me feel like I hit the jackpot when it comes to extended family; to Jonathan Parolini and all of my supportive friends, for letting me bounce ideas off you about the book; to Jim Wyatt, for the terrific advice and encouragement and for believing in my ability to take on this grand project; and finally, to all Tennessee Titans fans, for being the most passionate, loyal, and dedicated fan base in sports.

Edited by Ryan Jacobson. Proofread by Emily Beaumont. Fact-checked by Chris Zobin. Cover logo by Madhusanka. Background garnish by Y. Shane Nitzsche. Interior design by Ryan Jacobson and Y. Shane Nitzsche.

Eddie George photograph (front cover) by Al Messerschmidt Archive. Copyright 2024 The Associated Press. Football photograph (back cover) by Billion Photos/Shutterstock.com. Football helmet (spine) by RazorGraphix/ Shutterstock.com. For additional photography credits, see page 172.

10 9 8 7 6 5 4 3 2 1

Published by Lake 7 Creative, LLC
Minneapolis, MN 55412
www.lake7creative.com

Printed in China

ISBN: 978-1-960084-31-6

FOOTBALL ABBREVIATIONS

AFC: American Football Conference

AFL: American Football League

C: Center

CB: Cornerback

CFL: Canadian Football League

DB: Defensive back

DE: Defensive end

DT: Defensive tackle

FL: Flanker

FS: Free safety

FB: Fullback

G: Guard

HB: Halfback

K: Kicker

KR: Kick returner

LB: Linebacker

LE: Left end

LG: Left guard

LH: Left halfback

LS: Long snapper

LT: Left tackle

MLB: Middle linebacker

MVP: Most valuable player

NFC: National Football Conference

NFL: National Football League

NT: Nose tackle

OLB: Outside linebacker

OT: Offensive tackle / Overtime

P: Punter

PR: Punt returner

QB: Quarterback

RB: Running back

RE: Right end

RG: Right guard

RH: Right halfback

RT: Right tackle

T: Tackle

TE: Tight end

S: Safety

SS: Strong safety

ST: Special teams

UDFA: Undrafted free agent

USFL: United States Football League

WR: Wide receiver

Starting Lineup

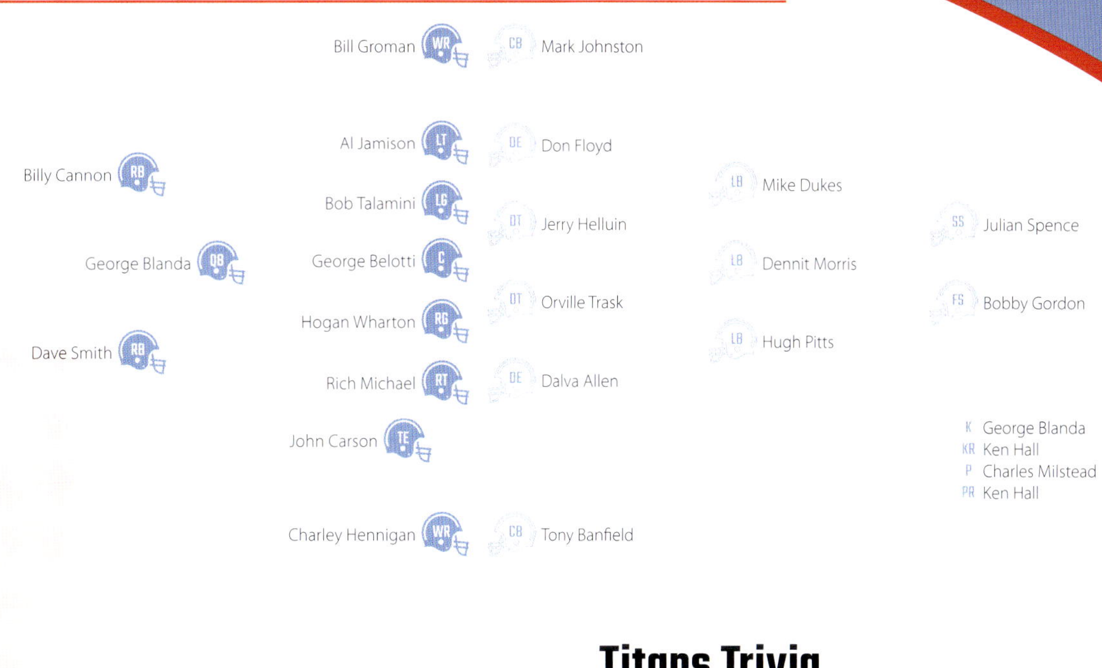

Titans Trivia

Bill Groman's 1,473 receiving yards stood as a single-season record among rookie wideouts until it was broken by Puca Nacua in 2023.

Pro Bowl Selections

- Al Jamison (OT)
- Mark Johnston (CB)
- Dave Smith (RB)

FOREWORD

As a Nashville native, I consider myself extremely fortunate to write for the city's NFL team, the Tennessee Titans.

Growing up, and in my early years working for *The Tennessean,* I viewed professional sports from afar. I thought it would always be that way.

Then came rumors of the Houston Oilers moving to Nashville.

What seemed like a pipe dream eventually became reality, when the Houston Oilers became the Tennessee Oilers—and then the Tennessee Titans.

A lot has transpired in Tennessee since, from the first year at the Liberty Bowl in Memphis to the team playing at Vanderbilt Stadium to the move to Adelphia Coliseum in 1999, when the Titans made a memorable run to Super Bowl XXXIV.

Time has sure flown by, like a Steve McNair pass.

When my friend Justin Melo informed me that he was working on *Titans of the South,* I knew it would be quite an undertaking, covering ground from Eddie George to Chris Johnson to Derrick Henry.

He then informed me he'd go all the way back to 1960, the first year of the franchise, the old AFL days, when owner K.S. "Bud" Adams founded the organization. Back then, stars like George Blanda, Jim Norton, Elvin Bethea, Robert Brazile, Earl Campbell, Ken Houston, Charlie Joiner, Mike Munchak, Warren Moon, Curley Culp, and Bruce Matthews put the Oilers on the map.

The spotlight shifted to McNair, George, Johnson, Henry, and countless more in Tennessee, where the franchise made a lasting impression with the Music City Miracle. I was lucky enough to be on hand for that and for every Titans game that's ever been played at what's now called Nissan Stadium.

When Justin shared some of his work before sending it to the publisher, I was intrigued and impressed.

The coffee-table book about the Houston Oilers/Tennessee Titans—with vivid color photographs and a comprehensive look at the team's history, from its legendary players to its monumental victories—should be a must-read for fans of the organization.

I've gotten to know Justin over the years and have been impressed with his work ethic and devotion. As a writer, podcaster, and reporter, Justin has established himself in many areas while covering the NFL and the Titans.

His passion for the Titans—and his work—are abundantly clear in this book, which includes photos, stats, schedules, starting lineups, and a summary of each season. This book also includes all-decade teams.

Reading this book brought back a lot of memories for me and also told me plenty I didn't know.

—Jim Wyatt
Senior Writer and Editor
of TennesseeTitans.com

INTRODUCTION

"Maybe we ought to start our own league."

Those were the words that Kenneth Stanley "Bud" Adams, Jr., allegedly uttered to Lamar Hunt while the two shrewd businessmen bonded at dinner over their failure to buy a controlling interest in the Chicago Cardinals. By the time the forward-thinking men saw each other again, Hunt had lined up five franchises for Adams' proposed league, including his hometown Dallas Texans. Adams added the Houston Oilers, and, in 1960, the American Football League (AFL) was born—a rival to the National Football League (NFL).

This book, *Titans of the South,* covers everything that has transpired since the inception of the Oilers/Titans franchise.

The first time I ever caught a football game on television, the Tennessee Titans were playing. I remember saying to myself, "Steve McNair and Eddie George are two excellent players. I could get used to watching this team play on Sundays." I've been glued to the television for every game since.

I was a preteen during the glory days of McNair and George, but the foundation was laid for a lifetime of fandom. All the franchise's dealings have captured my attention since. I am invested in the team's successes and failures, both on and off the field. I have learned everything I could about the history of Oilers/Titans football, from the very beginning. That led me to a successful career in sports journalism, covering the Titans via stories and podcasts—which then led me to write this book.

Every era of Oilers/Titans football is fascinating in its own right. I hope this book becomes your go-to resource for recalling the year-to-year happenings of the franchise.

Titan Up!

—Justin Melo

ABOUT BUD ADAMS

A native of Bartlesville, Oklahoma, Bud Adams founded the original Houston Oilers franchise that would controversially move to Tennessee in the late 1990s. Adams had his fair share of rifts with front office executives, his own coaches, and even competing owners. Through all the ups and downs, he remained committed to bringing championship football to Houston and Nashville.

Adams was the son of K. S. "Boots" Adams and Blanch Keeler Adams. His father was named president of Phillips Petroleum Company in 1938. In 1947, Bud Adams founded the ADA Oil Company, a wholesale supplier of oil and natural gas that became the foundation of his fortune. It eventually developed into Adams Resources and Energy, Inc., which went public in 1974. Adams served as the company's chief executive officer for more than half a century.

On October 21, 2013, Adams died of natural causes at the age of 90. Ownership of the team was then split between his daughters Amy Adams Strunk and Susie Adams Smith; his daughter-in-law, Susan Lewis, the widow of Adams' late son Kenneth S. Adams III (who passed away in 1987); and his grandchildren (Susan's sons) Kenneth S. Adams IV and Barclay Adams. Following two tumultuous seasons, Amy Adams Strunk became the sole controlling owner in 2015, a role she proudly maintains as of this publication.

The Titans play in Nissan Stadium. A new stadium is set to open in 2027.

TABLE OF CONTENTS

A BIT OF NFL HISTORY

The Houston Oilers were charter members of the American Football League (AFL), and the franchise was founded in 1960. The Boston Patriots, Buffalo Bills, and New York Titans joined Houston as the original teams in the AFL East Division. In 1966, the Miami Dolphins were added to the division.

The AFL and the National Football League (NFL) merged in 1970, and the Oilers competed in the American Football Conference (AFC) Central Division, along with the Cincinnati Bengals, Cleveland Browns, and Pittsburgh Steelers.

The Oilers relocated to Tennessee in 1997 and became the Tennessee Oilers. Two years later, in 1999, the franchise adopted the Tennessee Titans moniker—a name associated with Greek mythology and a nod to Nashville's reputation as "Athens of the South." The Titans remained in the AFC Central until the NFL realigned the divisions in 2002. The Titans, Houston Texans, Indianapolis Colts, and Jacksonville Jaguars have made up the AFC South ever since.

From 1960 to 1977, the team played a 14-game schedule each season. That was expanded to 16 games per season, beginning in 1978. The two exceptions were in 1982 (nine games) and 1987 (15 games), when the schedules were shortened by labor disputes. The NFL expanded to a 17-game schedule beginning in 2021.

AUTHOR'S NOTES

Pro Bowl: All Pro Bowl selections include original ballot picks as recognized by the Tennessee Titans Media Guide. AFL All-Stars are designated as Pro Bowl selections. In 1960, there were no AFL All-Stars; the players listed were All-Pro.

Key Additions: A key part of telling the season-by-season story of the Houston Oilers/Tennessee Titans comes from spotlighting the most influential players added on a yearly basis. The selections I've included are subjective, based on overall impact, tenure, and achievements with the organization.

Sacks: The NFL did not make sacks an official statistic until 1982. Any sack numbers referenced before 1982 are courtesy of Pro Football Reference.

Starting Lineups: Identifying the starting lineup of any given season is a tricky task. Inevitable injuries and player rotations have an impact on the lineups. With that in mind, the players listed are—in most cases—recognized as the primary starters for that season by the official Tennessee Titans Media Guide. While I did my best, the alignments aren't perfect. For example, wide receivers might not be listed on their most typical side of the field. However, the starting lineups should give you a good idea of which players had the biggest impacts at their respective positions.

1960

10–4

First in AFL East, AFL Champions

The inaugural roster of the Houston Oilers was a perfect mix of experienced players from other professional leagues and talented rookies. Four-time All-America Football Conference (AAFC) champion Lou Rymkus was named the first head coach in team history, and former basketball coach Don Suman was the general manager. The Oilers played their home games at Jeppesen Stadium in Houston.

Louisiana State University halfback Billy Cannon was the first draft selection in Oilers history. Cannon, along with quarterback George Blanda and wide receiver Bill Groman emerged as playmakers for Houston's high-flying offense. The Oilers scored 379 points, the second most in the American Football League (AFL). Groman led the league in receiving yards (1,473) and in yards per reception (20.5). Wide receiver Charley Hennigan scored the first touchdown in team history—via a 43-yard pass from Blanda—in the first quarter of Houston's Week 1 game against the Oakland Raiders.

The 1960 Oilers were a balanced unit with a stingy defense. They possessed the league's second-ranked scoring defense, allowing just 285 points, or 20.3 points per contest. They held their opponents to 14 points or less on four occasions.

The Oilers stated their championship intentions by jumping to a 5–1 record. The team clinched the AFL East Division title with a 31–23 victory over the Buffalo Bills, and they advanced to face the Los Angeles Chargers in the first AFL Championship Game.

Nursing a 17–16 lead entering the fourth quarter, Blanda located Cannon for a highlight-reel 88-yard touchdown catch-and-run to extend the lead to eight. The score held, and Houston won the championship, 24–16. Cannon finished with 50 rushing yards and 128 receiving yards, and he was named the game's Most Valuable Player (MVP).

Rymkus was voted the AFL's inaugural Coach of the Year, a much-deserved honor for one of the more successful seasons in franchise history. Additional success would immediately follow.

Schedule

	OPPONENT	SCORE	RECORD
W	@ Oakland Raiders	37–22	1–0
W	Los Angeles Chargers	38–28	2–0
L	Oakland Raiders	13–14	2–1
W	New York Titans	27–21	3–1
W	Dallas Texans	20–10	4–1
W	@ New York Titans	42–28	5–1
L	@ Buffalo Bills	24–25	5–2
W	@ Denver Broncos	45–25	6–2
L	@ Los Angeles Chargers	21–24	6–3
W	Denver Broncos	20–10	7–3
W	@ Boston Patriots	24–10	8–3
L	@ Dallas Texans	0–24	8–4
W	Buffalo Bills	31–23	9–4
W	Boston Patriots	37–21	10–4
W	*Los Angeles Chargers*	*24–16*	*1–0*

Season Leaders

CATEGORY	TOTAL	PLAYER
Passing Yards	2,413	George Blanda
Rushing Yards	644	Billy Cannon
Receiving Yards	1,473	Bill Groman
Receptions	72	Bill Groman
Interceptions	4	Johnston, Morris, Spence
Sacks	5	Don Floyd
Points	115	George Blanda

Key Additions:
George Blanda (QB), Billy Cannon (RB), Don Floyd (DE), Charley Hennigan (WR), Jim Norton (CB), Bob Talamini (G)

1961

10–3–1

First in AFL East, AFL Champions

The Oilers' title-defending campaign began in lackluster fashion. A championship hangover was evident as the team crawled out of the gate to a 1–3–1 record. Following a 31–31 tie with the Boston Patriots, owner Bud Adams made one of his boldest moves. He fired Lou Rymkus, reigning AFL Coach of the Year, who had led the Oilers to a championship the season prior. Adams replaced Rymkus with Wally Lemm, who had served as an assistant defensive coach for Houston in 1960. Adams' gamble turned out to be one of his best football decisions.

Coach Lemm immediately righted the ship. The Oilers averaged 41.1 points per game under his direction, while embarking on a nine-game winning streak to conclude the regular season. The winning streak included a 55–14 victory over the Denver Broncos. Dual-threat running back Billy Cannon rushed for 118 yards and a score, and he tallied 68 receiving yards and a receiving touchdown. Wide receiver Bill Groman added 134 receiving yards and scored three touchdowns.

Lemm's success saw the Oilers capture a second consecutive AFL East title, setting up a rematch with the Chargers (who moved to San Diego) in the AFL Championship. Houston fielded the league's highest-scoring offense, but the game was a defensive struggle. Sloppy play from both sides led to a combined 13 turnovers. The Oilers nursed a 3–0 lead at halftime, thanks to a 46-yard field goal by George Blanda. The lone touchdown was scored during the third quarter. Facing third-and-five in San Diego territory, Blanda rolled right and located Cannon for a 35-yard touchdown connection. The Chargers avoided a shutout by hitting a fourth-quarter field goal, but the Oilers won their second straight AFL championship, 10–3.

It was arguably the greatest season in Oilers history. Blanda led the league in passing yards (3,330) and passing touchdowns (36). Cannon won the rushing title (948). Charley Hennigan led all wideouts in receiving yards (1,746), and Bill Groman led all pass-catchers in receiving touchdowns (17). The Oilers scored a league-high 36.6 points per game. Their 513 total points came in 100 points more than the next best team (Boston Patriots, 413). Blanda was named the AFL Player of the Year.

Schedule

	OPPONENT	SCORE	RECORD
W	Oakland Raiders	55–0	1–0
L	@ San Diego Chargers	24–34	1–1
L	@ Dallas Texans	21–26	1–2
L	Buffalo Bills	12–22	1–3
T	@ Boston Patriots	31–31	1–3–1
W	Dallas Texans	38–7	2–3–1
W	@ Buffalo Bills	28–16	3–3–1
W	@ Denver Broncos	55–14	4–3–1
W	Boston Patriots	27–15	5–3–1
W	New York Titans	49–13	6–3–1
W	Denver Broncos	45–14	7–3–1
W	San Diego Chargers	33–13	8–3–1
W	@ New York Titans	48–21	9–3–1
W	@ Oakland Raiders	47–16	10–3–1
W	*@ San Diego Chargers*	*10–3*	*1–0*

Season Leaders

CATEGORY	TOTAL	PLAYER
Passing Yards	3,330	George Blanda
Rushing Yards	948	Billy Cannon
Receiving Yards	1,746	Charley Hennigan
Receptions	82	Charley Hennigan
Interceptions	9	Jim Norton
Sacks	8	Ed Husmann
Points	112	George Blanda

Key Additions:
Fred Glick (S), Ed Husmann (OT), Bob Schmidt (C), Charley Tolar (RB)

Starting Lineup

Bill Groman WR — CB Mark Johnston

Al Jamison LT — DE Don Floyd

Bob Talamini LG — DT Ed Husmann

Bob Schmidt C — DT Orville Trask

Hogan Wharton RG — DE Dalva Allen

Rich Michael RT

Bob McLeod TE

Charley Hennigan WR — CB Tony Banfield

Billy Cannon RB

George Blanda QB

Charley Tolar RB

LB Mike Dukes

LB Dennit Morris

LB Doug Cline

SS Jim Norton

FS Fred Glick

K George Blanda
KR Billy Cannon
P Jim Norton
PR Billy Cannon

Titans Trivia

Willard Dewveall (TE/WR) joined the Oilers in 1961. Coming from the Bears, he became the first player to move from the NFL to the AFL.

Pro Bowl Selections

- Tony Banfield (CB)
- George Blanda (QB)
- Billy Cannon (RB)
- Don Floyd (DE)
- Charley Hennigan (WR)
- Ed Husmann (DT)
- Al Jamison (OT)
- Mark Johnston (S)
- Bob McLeod (TE)
- Dennit Morris (LB)
- Bob Schmidt (C)
- Charley Tolar (RB)

Back-to-Back Champs

Winning the AFL East in 1960 meant the Oilers advanced to face the Los Angeles Chargers in the first AFL Championship Game, played at Jeppesen Stadium on January 1, 1961. The Chargers opened the scoring with a pair of field goals in the first quarter. The Oilers answered with 10 points, including a 17-yard touchdown pass from quarterback George Blanda to running back Dave Smith. Los Angeles added a field goal before halftime, and Houston held a slim lead, 10–9.

A seven-yard scoring pass from Blanda to wide receiver Bill Groman extended the lead for Houston, but Los Angeles responded with a touchdown drive of their own. The only points in the fourth quarter came on an astounding 88-yard touchdown catch-and-run by star running back Billy Cannon. Houston won the AFL championship, 24–16.

A year later, on December 24, 1961, the same two teams squared off again—this time at Balboa Stadium in San Diego. (The Chargers had moved from Los Angeles.) Unlike the first meeting, this championship game was a defensive struggle. Blanda threw five interceptions, and Groman threw another. On top of that, the Oilers fumbled five times but were fortunate to recover four of them. On the other side of the ball, San Diego turned over the football six times.

The only scoring in the first half was a 46-yard Blanda field goal, gifted to Houston after a nine-yard Chargers punt. In the third quarter, the Oilers strung together the only sustained drive of the game by either team: an 80-yarder that ended with a 35-yard touchdown catch by Cannon. San Diego added a field goal in the fourth, but with each offense gaining just 256 yards, the sloppily played game ended in Houston's favor, 10–3.

In two championship games, Billy Cannon gained 279 yards from scrimmage and scored two touchdowns.

56
20

1962

11–3
First in AFL East

After leading Houston to a championship in 1961, Wally Lemm resigned as head coach during the offseason. Lemm chose to pursue other opportunities, and he was eventually named head coach of the National Football League's Saint Louis Cardinals. Lemm was replaced in Houston by Frank "Pop" Ivy, who coincidentally had coached the Cardinals in 1961—so the Oilers and Cardinals essentially swapped coaches.

Houston's 1962 campaign got off to an up-and-down start as the players acclimated to Ivy's coaching methods. A 4–3 midseason record didn't suggest that the Oilers were en route to a third straight championship game. That's when everything began clicking.

The Oilers ended the regular season on a seven-game winning streak. That effort helped them capture a third consecutive AFL East title and set them up for a third straight appearance in the AFL Championship Game. This time, the Oilers locked horns with the Dallas Texans in what became an instant classic.

The Texans dominated the first half, commanding a 17–0 halftime lead. But Houston mounted a second-half comeback. Quarterback George Blanda found Willard Dewveall for a 15-yard score to get the Oilers on the board. Then, in the fourth quarter, Blanda hit a 31-yard field goal, and Charley Tolar scored a one-yard rushing touchdown to complete the comeback and tie the game, 17–17. In the dying moments of the fourth quarter, Blanda kicked what would have been a 42-yard game-winning field goal, but it was blocked.

Overtime came and went, and so did multiple squandered opportunities by both teams. In the second overtime, Texans rookie kicker Tommy Brooker connected on a 25-yard field goal to clinch the Texans' first AFL championship.

As painful as the defeat to their in-state rivals was, the Oilers would face darker days ahead. The 1962 campaign represented the conclusion of Houston's three-year dominance over their AFL competitors. Things went downhill quickly for this championship-caliber team.

Schedule

	OPPONENT	SCORE	RECORD
W	@ Buffalo Bills	28–23	1–0
L	@ Boston Patriots	21–34	1–1
W	@ San Diego Chargers	42–17	2–1
W	Buffalo Bills	17–14	3–1
W	New York Titans	56–17	4–1
L	@ Denver Broncos	10–20	4–2
L	Dallas Texans	7–31	4–3
W	@ Dallas Texans	14–6	5–3
W	@ Oakland Raiders	28–20	6–3
W	Boston Patriots	21–17	7–3
W	San Diego Chargers	33–27	8–3
W	Denver Broncos	34–17	9–3
W	Oakland Raiders	32–17	10–3
W	@ New York Titans	44–10	11–3
L	*Dallas Texans (OT)*	*17–20*	*0–1*

Season Leaders

CATEGORY	TOTAL	PLAYER
Passing Yards	2,810	George Blanda
Rushing Yards	1,012	Charley Tolar
Receiving Yards	867	Charley Hennigan
Receptions	54	Charley Hennigan
Interceptions	8	Jim Norton
Sacks	10	Ed Husmann
Points	81	George Blanda

Key Additions:
Gary Cutsinger (DE), Bobby Jancik (DB)

Starting Lineup

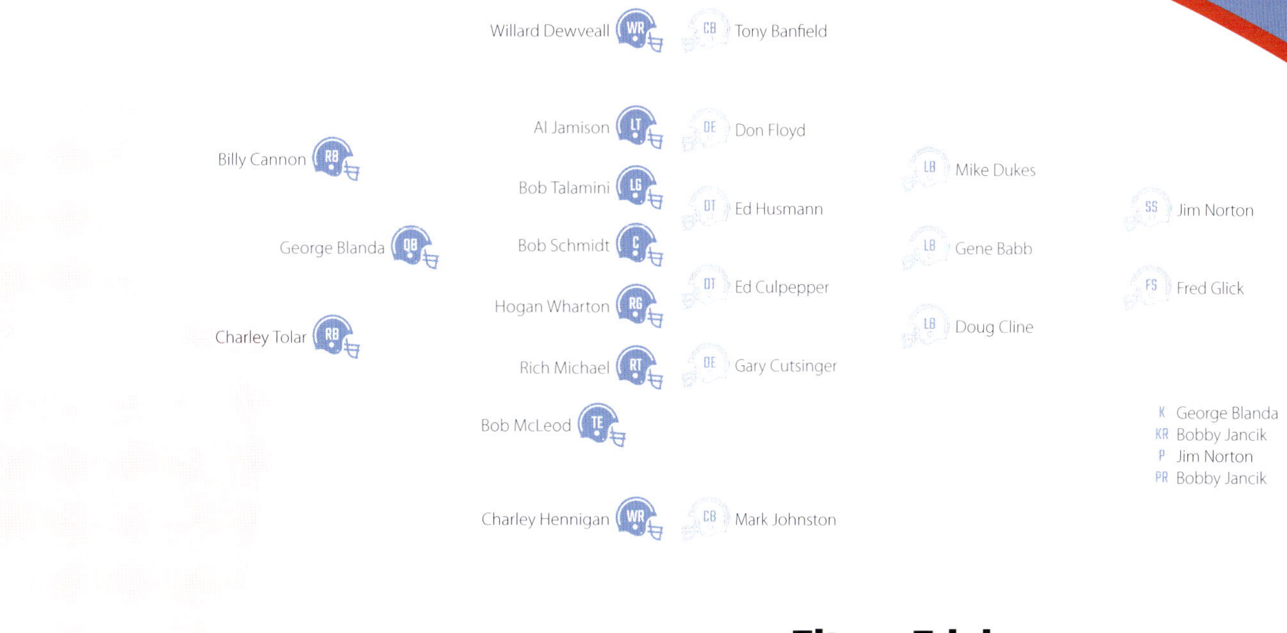

Titans Trivia

George Blanda threw 42 interceptions in 1962, a single-season record that still stands.

Pro Bowl Selections

- Tony Banfield (CB)
- George Blanda (QB)
- Willard Dewveall (WR)
- Don Floyd (DE)
- Fred Glick (S)
- Charley Hennigan (WR)
- Ed Husmann (DT)
- Al Jamison (OT)
- Rich Michael (OT)
- Jim Norton (S)
- Bob Schmidt (C)
- Bob Talamini (G)
- Charley Tolar (RB)

6–8
3rd in AFL East

Injuries and departures severely hampered the Houston Oilers—especially on offense—throughout the 1963 season. Head coach Frank "Pop" Ivy was given full control over personnel as the acting general manager, and he dealt with some challenges. Most notably, left tackle Al Jamison suffered a serious back injury and retired at the conclusion of the 1962 season.

Jamison wasn't the lone absentee that hurt Houston's offensive efforts. Wide receiver Bill Groman, who suffered a debilitating knee injury in 1962, moved on to play for the Denver Broncos. On top of that, recurring leg and back problems caused superstar running back Billy Cannon to miss much of the season. In his place, the Oilers leaned on Bill Tobin, Charley Tolar, and Dave Smith to lead their backfield.

The Oilers averaged a sixth-ranked 21.6 points per game. This marked the first time Houston's offense finished lower than second in the league. Quarterback George Blanda still led the league in passing yards with 3,003—but a seventh-ranked rushing attack led to a one-dimensional unit.

Still, at times, the inconsistent Oilers appeared capable of making their fourth consecutive appearance in the AFL Championship. A four-game winning streak improved their record to 5–3. However, they lost four straight contests to end the season with a third-place finish in the AFL East.

Fred Glick's 12 interceptions set a single-season franchise record. That record stood alone for nearly two decades, until Mike Reinfeldt recorded 12 interceptions during the 1979 season.

Pro Bowl Selections

- Tony Banfield (CB)
- George Blanda (QB)
- Fred Glick (S)
- Charley Hennigan (WR)
- Ed Husmann (DT)
- Rich Michael (OT)
- Jim Norton (S)
- Bob Schmidt (C)
- Bob Talamini (G)

Schedule

	OPPONENT	SCORE	RECORD
L	Oakland Raiders	13–24	0–1
W	Denver Broncos	20–14	1–2
L	@ New York Jets	17–24	1–2
W	@ Buffalo Bills	31–20	2–2
L	@ Kansas City Chiefs	7–28	2–3
W	@ Denver Broncos	33–24	3–3
W	Buffalo Bills	28–14	4–3
W	Kansas City Chiefs	28–7	5–3
L	@ Boston Patriots	3–45	5–4
W	New York Jets	31–27	6–4
L	@ San Diego Chargers	0–27	6–5
L	Boston Patriots	28–46	6–6
L	San Diego Chargers	14–20	6–7
L	@ Oakland Raiders	49–52	6–8

Season Leaders

CATEGORY	TOTAL	PLAYER
Passing Yards	3,003	George Blanda
Rushing Yards	659	Charley Tolar
Receiving Yards	1,051	Charley Hennigan
Receptions	61	Charley Hennigan
Interceptions	12	Fred Glick
Sacks	5	G. Cutsinger, E. Husmann
Points	66	George Blanda

Key Additions:
None

Starting Lineup

OFFENSE	POSITION
George Blanda	QB
Bill Tobin	RB
Charley Tolar	RB
Willard Dewveall	WR
Charley Hennigan	WR
Bob McLeod	TE
Walt Suggs	LT
Bob Talamini	LG
Bob Schmidt	C
Hogan Wharton	RG
Rich Michael	RT

DEFENSE	POSITION
Gary Cutsinger	DE
Dudley Meredith	DT
Ed Husmann	DT
Don Floyd	DE
Doug Cline	OLB
Gene Babb	MLB
Mike Dukes	OLB
Tony Banfield	CB
Bobby Jancik	CB
Jim Norton	SS
Fred Glick	FS

SPECIAL TEAMS	POSITION
George Blanda	K
Bobby Jancik	KR
Jim Norton	P
Fred Glick	PR

In 98 games with Houston, George Blanda threw 165 touchdowns and 189 interceptions.

1964

4–10
Fourth in AFL East

Acting general manager and head coach Frank "Pop" Ivy was relieved of his duties following a lackluster 1963 campaign. Assistant general manager Carroll Martin was promoted to GM. Sammy Baugh, who had previously coached the New York Titans, was named the Oilers head coach.

A new regime couldn't get the Oilers back on track. The team regressed in 1964, going from 6–8 to a franchise-worst 4–10. Martin and Baugh struggled to navigate through changes in on-field personnel.

Superstar running back Billy Cannon, who had dealt with leg and back injuries in 1962 and 1963, requested a trade out of Houston. He was sent to the Oakland Raiders in exchange for offensive lineman Sonny Bishop, fullback Bobby Jackson, and halfback Dobie Craig. Cannon was replaced by rookie draft pick Sid Blanks.

Sweeping changes also occurred across the offensive line. Three-year starting center Bob Schmidt was replaced by reserve Tom Goode, while four-year starting right guard Hogan Wharton was replaced by John Wittenborn. Finally, Bishop, who was acquired from the Raiders in the Cannon deal, took over for four-year starter Rich Michael at right tackle.

The mainstays did their best to navigate the Oilers through their offensive challenges. Quarterback George Blanda finished second in the league in passing yards with 3,287. Wide receiver Charley Hennigan recorded a franchise-best 101 receptions, a single-season AFL record.

Defensive changes were felt throughout the lineup. Rookie first-round pick Scott Appleton recorded two sacks. A new ballhawk emerged in rookie defensive back Pete Jaquess, who led the team in interceptions with eight. It wasn't enough to prevent the Oilers from fielding the league's second-worst scoring defense, allowing 25.4 points per game.

It was a disappointing season overall. Baugh stepped down as head coach prior to Houston's season-finale victory over the Denver Broncos. That contest was the team's final game at Jeppesen Stadium, which the Oilers had called home since their inception in 1960.

Schedule

	OPPONENT	SCORE	RECORD
L	@ San Diego Chargers	21–27	0–1
W	Oakland Raiders	42–28	1–1
W	@ Denver Broncos	38–17	2–1
L	@ Kansas City Chiefs	7–28	2–2
L	Buffalo Bills	17–48	2–3
L	@ New York Jets	21–24	2–4
L	San Diego Chargers	17–20	2–5
L	@ Buffalo Bills	10–24	2–6
L	@ Boston Patriots	24–25	2–7
L	@ Oakland Raiders	10–20	2–8
L	Kansas City Chiefs	19–28	2–9
L	Boston Patriots	17–34	2–10
W	New York Jets	33–17	3–10
W	Denver Broncos	34–15	4–10

Season Leaders

CATEGORY	TOTAL	PLAYER
Passing Yards	3,287	George Blanda
Rushing Yards	756	Sid Blanks
Receiving Yards	1,546	Charley Hennigan
Receptions	101	Charley Hennigan
Interceptions	8	Pete Jaquess
Sacks	4	D. Floyd, E. Husmann
Points	76	George Blanda

Key Additions:
Sonny Bishop (OT), Sid Blanks (RB), W.K. Hicks (S), Pete Jaquess (CB)

Starting Lineup

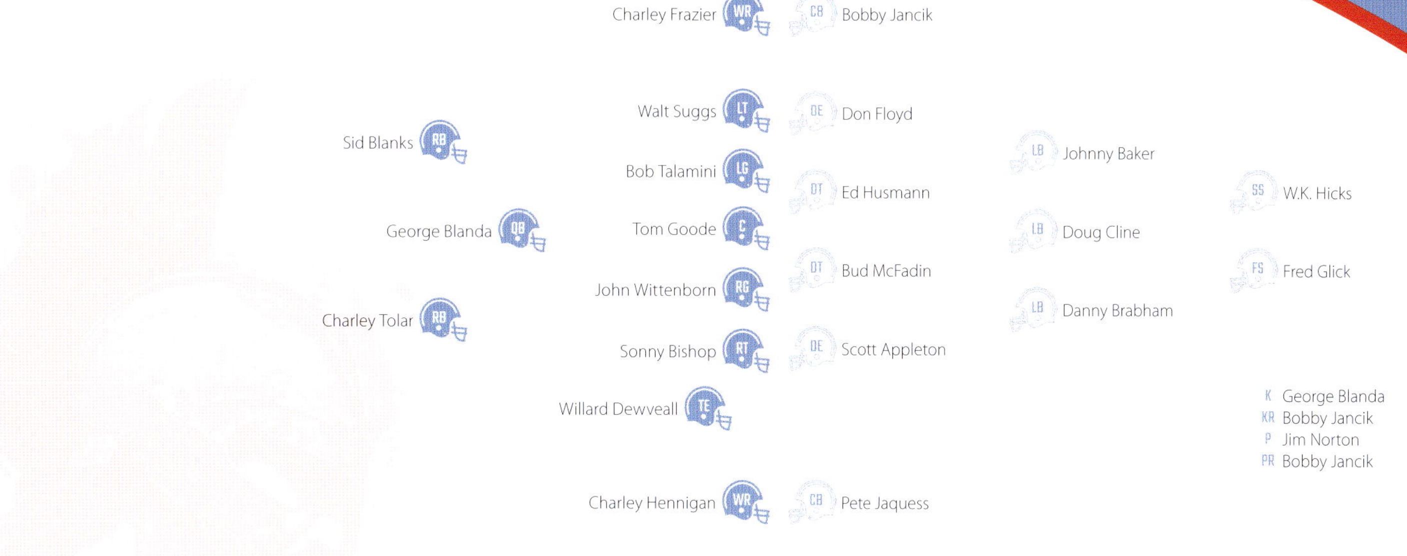

Titans Trivia

Sid Blanks played college football at Texas A&I. He was the first African-American to compete in the Lone Star Conference.

Pro Bowl Selections

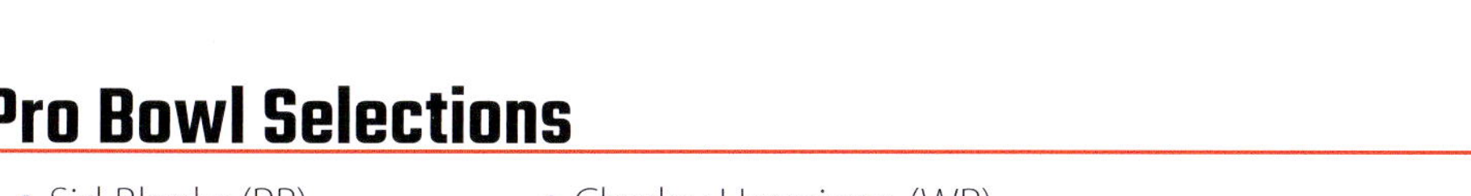

- Sid Blanks (RB)
- Don Floyd (DE)
- Fred Glick (S)
- Charley Hennigan (WR)
- Pete Jaquess (CB)
- Bob Talamini (G)

1965

4–10
Fourth in AFL East

The Oilers moved out of Jeppesen Stadium ahead of the 1965 campaign. The franchise was planning to play their home games at the Harris County Domed Stadium, but that deal fell apart. The team cited an "unrealistic lease agreement" as the reason. Owner Bud Adams avoided disaster by brokering a deal for his Oilers to play at Rice University's home stadium.

During the 1964 season, head coach Sammy Baugh had stepped down with one game remaining, but he oddly stayed on the staff as an offensive assistant in 1965. Baugh was replaced as head coach by Hugh "Bones" Taylor, who had served as an assistant on Baugh's staff. Taylor had played for Washington from 1947 to 1954 and was an assistant coach in the AFL from 1960 to 1964.

As a first-time head coach, Taylor failed to rejuvenate the Oilers. Running back Sid Blanks suffered a season-ending knee injury in training camp and missed the entire campaign. He was replaced by the multipurpose Ode Burrell, who led the offense in rushing yards (528) and finished second in receiving yards (650).

The Oilers were a promising 4–3 through seven games. A disappointing seven-game losing streak derailed the campaign. Taylor's offense failed to score more than 21 points in six of those contests.

The team finished an abysmal 4–10 for a second consecutive season. Houston's run defense was especially poor. The Oilers allowed an astounding 5.29 rushing yards per carry.

These Oilers were forgettable. The head coach was dismissed at the end of the season. General manager Carroll Martin also left the team. Martin joined new league commissioner Al Davis in the AFL's front office.

Sweeping changes were on the horizon, including one historical announcement that would shake the foundation of professional football. The landscape would never be the same.

Schedule

	OPPONENT	SCORE	RECORD
W	New York Jets	27–21	1–0
W	Boston Patriots	31–10	2–0
L	@ Oakland Raiders	17–21	2–1
L	@ San Diego Chargers	14–31	2–2
L	@ Denver Broncos	17–28	2–3
W	Kansas City Chiefs	38–36	3–3
W	@ Buffalo Bills	19–17	4–3
L	Oakland Raiders	21–33	4–4
L	Denver Broncos	21–31	4–5
L	@ New York Jets	14–41	4–6
L	@ Kansas City Chiefs	21–52	4–7
L	Buffalo Bills	18–29	4–8
L	San Diego Chargers	26–37	4–9
L	@ Boston Patriots	14–42	4–10

Season Leaders

CATEGORY	TOTAL	PLAYER
Passing Yards	2,542	George Blanda
Rushing Yards	528	Ode Burrell
Receiving Yards	717	Charley Frazier
Receptions	55	Ode Burrell
Interceptions	9	W.K. Hicks
Sacks	7	Gary Cutsinger
Points	61	George Blanda

Key Additions:
Bobby Maples (LB)

Starting Lineup

Titans Trivia

5.29 rushing yards allowed per carry was the worst season total in AFL history and the eighth-worst in professional football history.

Pro Bowl Selections

- Ode Burrell (RB)
- Willie Frazier (TE)
- Charley Hennigan (WR)
- Bob Talamini (G)

1966

3–11
Fourth in AFL East

Owner Bud Adams hired a new executive vice president and general manager: Don Klosterman, a former quarterback whose playing career was cut short by a life-threatening ski accident. Together, Adams and Klosterman began reshaping the Oilers. For starters, they hired Wally Lemm to be the head coach. Lemm had previously coached the Oilers in 1961, taking over the team midway through the season and helping the Oilers capture their second consecutive league championship.

Lemm's return to the team was a popular move among fans, and his 1966 Oilers got off to a quick start. They defeated the Denver Broncos, 45–7, in the regular-season opener. The Broncos were held to zero first downs, an AFL defensive record. In their second contest, the Oilers shut out the Oakland Raiders, 31–0. It was all downhill from there.

After dropping three of their next four games, Lemm's Oilers finished the season on an eight-game losing streak to clinch a franchise-worst record of 3–11. A lack of stability at quarterback helped to derail the season. The Oilers started three different quarterbacks in 1966: George Blanda (eight), Don Trull (five), and Buddy Humphrey (one).

On June 8, 1966, prior to the season's start, an announcement was made that shocked the football world. The AFL and NFL announced plans to merge into one league by 1970. Dallas Cowboys (NFL) general manager Tex Schramm and AFL co-founder Lamar Hunt (Dallas Texans/Kansas City Chiefs) were instrumental throughout the discussions that eventually led to a merger agreement.

Under the agreement, the leagues would maintain separate regular-season schedules for the next four campaigns—from 1966 through 1969—and then officially merge prior to the 1970 season to form a larger, ultra-competitive league. The leagues also agreed to play an annual AFL-NFL World Championship Game beginning with the 1966 season, which would become known as the Super Bowl. The AFL had been successful in its efforts to compete with the NFL. Now, professional football found itself on the verge of achieving sports dominance.

Schedule

	OPPONENT	SCORE	RECORD
W	Denver Broncos	45–7	1–0
W	Oakland Raiders	31–0	2–0
L	@ New York Jets	13–52	2–1
L	@ Buffalo Bills	20–27	2–2
L	@ Denver Broncos	38–40	2–3
W	New York Jets	24–0	3–3
L	Miami Dolphins	13–20	3–4
L	@ Kansas City Chiefs	23–48	3–5
L	@ Oakland Raiders	23–38	3–6
L	@ Boston Patriots	21–27	3–7
L	Buffalo Bills	20–42	3–8
L	San Diego Chargers	22–28	3–9
L	Boston Patriots	14–38	3–10
L	@ Miami Dolphins	28–29	3–11

Season Leaders

CATEGORY	TOTAL	PLAYER
Passing Yards	1,764	George Blanda
Rushing Yards	406	Ode Burrell
Receiving Yards	1,129	Charley Frazier
Receptions	57	Charley Frazier
Interceptions	4	Fred Glick, Jim Norton
Sacks	5.5	Gary Cutsinger
Points	87	George Blanda

Key Additions:
Hoyle Granger (RB), Pat Holmes (DT), Glen Ray Hines (OT)

Starting Lineup

Titans Trivia

The AFL expanded to nine teams in 1966 by adding the Miami Dolphins. Two bye weeks were added to navigate schedule changes.

Pro Bowl Selections

- Charley Frazier (WR)
- W.K. Hicks (CB)
- Bob Talamini (G)

1967

9-4-1

First in AFL East

There were significant personnel-related developments ahead of Wally Lemm's second full season as head coach: Star wide receiver Charley Hennigan retired, and the Oilers released legendary quarterback George Blanda.

At times, Houston struggled to navigate past Blanda's departure. They tried three different starting quarterbacks throughout their 14-game schedule. Jacky Lee, who had previously split time with Blanda, started the first three games. Rookie quarterback Bob Davis got the nod for Houston's next two contests. The team finally landed on Pete Beathard, who started the rest of the season.

Beathard was acquired in October from the Kansas City Chiefs in exchange for Lee and defensive tackle Ernie Ladd. Beathard completed just 41% of his passing attempts and threw more interceptions (14) than touchdowns (9). Incredibly, the Oilers still enjoyed a successful season.

Their offensive efforts were sparked by fullback Hoyle Granger, who experienced a breakout campaign in 1967. He rushed for 1,194 yards and six touchdowns. A dual-threat playmaker, Granger also led the team in receptions (31) and receiving yards (300). He led the entire league in total yards from scrimmage (1,494).

The Oilers won six more games than the previous season and finished in first place in the AFL East. Houston's efforts were spearheaded by a top-ranked defense that allowed a league-low 14.2 points per game. The Oilers advanced to their fourth AFL Championship Game. Unfortunately, this one was never close. The Oilers were defeated, 40–7, by the Oakland Raiders.

Pro Bowl Selections

- Woody Campbell (RB)
- Miller Farr (CB)
- Hoyle Granger (RB)
- Pat Holmes (DE)
- Jim Norton (S)
- Walt Suggs (OT)
- Bob Talamini (G)
- George Webster (LB)

Schedule

	OPPONENT	SCORE	RECORD
L	Kansas City Chiefs	20–25	0–1
W	@ Buffalo Bills	20–3	1–1
L	@ San Diego Chargers	3–13	1–2
W	Denver Broncos	10–6	2–2
T	@ New York Jets	28–28	2–2–1
W	@ Kansas City Chiefs	24–19	3–2–1
W	Buffalo Bills	10–3	4–2–1
L	@ Boston Patriots	7–18	4–3–1
W	@ Denver Broncos	20–18	5–3–1
W	Boston Patriots	27–6	6–3–1
W	Miami Dolphins	17–14	7–3–1
L	Oakland Raiders	7–19	7–4–1
W	San Diego Chargers	24–17	8–4–1
W	@ Miami Dolphins	41–10	9–4–1
L	*@ Oakland Raiders*	*7–40*	*0–1*

Season Leaders

CATEGORY	TOTAL	PLAYER
Passing Yards	1,114	Pete Beathard
Rushing Yards	1,194	Hoyle Granger
Receiving Yards	300	Hoyle Granger
Receptions	31	Hoyle Granger
Interceptions	10	Miller Farr
Sacks	6.5	George Rice
Points	72	John Wittenborn

Key Additions:
Woody Campbell (RB), Miller Farr (CB), Ken Houston (S), Zeke Moore (CB), Alvin Reed (TE), George Webster (LB)

A stellar punter and safety, Jim Norton was a three-time All-Star.

Starting Lineup

OFFENSE	POSITION
Pete Beathard	QB
Woody Campbell	RB
Hoyle Granger	RB
Ode Burrell	WR
Charley Frazier	WR
Alvin Reed	TE
Walt Suggs	LT
Bob Talamini	LG
Bobby Maples	C
Sonny Bishop	RG
Glen Ray Hines	RT

DEFENSE	POSITION
Pat Holmes	DE
Willie Parker	DT
George Rice	DT
Bud Marshall	DE
George Webster	OLB
Garland Boyette	MLB
Olen Underwood	OLB
Miller Farr	CB
W.K. Hicks	CB
Ken Houston	SS
Jim Norton	FS

SPECIAL TEAMS	POSITION
John Wittenborn	K
Bobby Jancik	KR
Jim Norton	P
Larry Carwell	PR

1968

7–7

Second in AFL East

Fresh off an appearance in the AFL Championship, the Houston Oilers moved into their full-time home ahead of the 1968 campaign. Team owner Bud Adams settled the Oilers' short-term lease agreement with Rice University, where the Oilers had played the previous three seasons. The team moved into the Houston Astrodome, agreeing to share the stadium with Major League Baseball's Houston Astros. Some 45,083 fans watched Houston's debut in the stadium, a 26–21 loss to the Kansas City Chiefs in Week 1.

The offseason also saw an abundance of change to the Oilers roster. Long-time guard Bob Talamini was released and replaced by Tom Regner, who had been drafted in 1967. Defensive stalwart Don Floyd also played his final season with the Oilers in 1967. Floyd enjoyed an illustrious eight-year career with the franchise as a starting defensive end and is one of the Oilers' all-time great defensive linemen.

In the third round of the 1968 AFL Draft, general manager Don Klosterman selected defensive end Elvin Bethea out of North Carolina A&T. Bethea immediately captured a notable role on the Oilers defense and would go on to become one of the best players in franchise history.

For the third season in a row, the Oilers started three different quarterbacks. Pete Beathard earned seven of 14 starts. Bob Davis started three games, and Don Trull, who was in his second stint with the team, got four starts.

Safety Ken Houston earned the first of what would be 12 consecutive All-Star/Pro Bowl appearances. Yet, despite welcoming some new star power, the team finished 7–7. So much change led to a mediocre season.

Pro Bowl Selections

- Sonny Bishop (G)
- Garland Boyette (LB)
- Miller Farr (CB)
- Hoyle Granger (RB)
- Glen Ray Hines (OT)
- Pat Holmes (DE)
- Bobby Maples (C)
- Alvin Reed (TE)
- Walt Suggs (OT)
- George Webster (LB)

Schedule

	OPPONENT	SCORE	RECORD
L	Kansas City Chiefs	21–26	0–1
W	@ Miami Dolphins	24–10	1–1
L	@ San Diego Chargers	14–30	1–2
L	Oakland Raiders	15–24	1–3
L	Miami Dolphins	7–24	1–4
W	@ Boston Patriots	16–0	2–4
L	New York Jets	14–20	2–5
W	@ Buffalo Bills	30–7	3–5
W	@ Cincinnati Bengals	27–17	4–5
L	@ New York Jets	7–26	4–6
W	Denver Broncos	38–17	5–6
L	@ Kansas City Chiefs	10–24	5–7
W	Buffalo Bills	35–6	6–7
W	Boston Patriots	45–17	7–7

Season Leaders

CATEGORY	TOTAL	PLAYER
Passing Yards	1,559	Pete Beathard
Rushing Yards	848	Hoyle Granger
Receiving Yards	747	Alvin Reed
Receptions	46	Alvin Reed
Interceptions	5	Ken Houston
Sacks	6.5	Pat Holmes
Points	50	Wayne Walker

Key Additions:
Elvin Bethea (DE)

Elvin Bethea was elected to the Pro Football Hall of Fame in 2003.

Starting Lineup

OFFENSE	POSITION
Pete Beathard	QB
Woody Campbell	RB
Hoyle Granger	RB
Mac Haik	WR
Jim Beirne	WR
Alvin Reed	TE
Walt Suggs	LT
Tom Regner	LG
Bobby Maples	C
Sonny Bishop	RG
Glen Ray Hines	RT

DEFENSE	POSITION
Pat Holmes	DE
Willie Parker	DT
George Rice	DT
Gary Cutsinger	DE
George Webster	OLB
Garland Boyette	MLB
Olen Underwood	OLB
Miller Farr	CB
Larry Carwell	CB
Ken Houston	SS
W.K. Hicks	FS

SPECIAL TEAMS	POSITION
Wayne Walker	K
Zeke Moore	KR
Jim Norton	P
Larry Carwell	PR

1969

6-6-2
Second in AFL East

Ahead of the Houston Oilers' 1969 campaign, the team put their hopes in ascending young talent as they parted ways with key veterans. Most notably, safety and punter Jim Norton announced his retirement. It represented the end of an era, as he was the last remaining Oiler from the original 1960 team. Norton's 45 career interceptions rank first in franchise history. He was inducted into the Oilers/Titans Hall of Fame in 1999, and his number 43 jersey was retired by the club.

Sophomore defensive end Elvin Bethea broke out of his shell. The former North Carolina A&T standout exploded for 14.5 sacks after enjoying modest success as a rookie. Another young star also emerged: The Oilers drafted wide receiver Charlie Joiner out of Grambling with a fourth-round pick in the 1969 AFL-NFL Draft. Joiner would go on to play the first three-plus seasons of his hall-of-fame career with the Oilers.

This final season before the AFL-NFL merger was productive for the Oilers. After ties in two consecutive games, Houston traveled to Miami to take on the Dolphins. The home team took a 7–0 lead, but the Oilers scored the final 32 points of the game.

Three weeks later, Houston entered their regular-season finale against the Boston Patriots with a 5–6–2 record, needing a victory to claim a postseason spot as the AFL East's second-place team. That scenario looked unlikely when the Patriots jumped to a 16–0 lead in the second quarter. But before halftime, quarterback Pete Beathard connected with wide receiver Alvin Reed for a 43-yard touchdown, giving the Oilers new life and stealing Boston's momentum.

The teams traded touchdowns in the third quarter, so Houston entered the fourth quarter down by two scores, 23–14. The Oilers tallied 13 unanswered points, spearheaded by a 13-yard touchdown pass from Beathard to wide receiver Jim Beirne. Houston triumphed with a thrilling 27–23 come-from-behind victory.

In the AFL's first and only divisional playoff round, Houston was dusted aside by the Oakland Raiders, 56–7, putting an end to their time in the AFL.

Schedule

	OPPONENT	SCORE	RECORD
L	@ Oakland Raiders	17–21	0–1
W	@ Buffalo Bills	17–3	1–1
W	Miami Dolphins	22–10	2–1
W	Buffalo Bills	28–14	3–1
L	@ Kansas City Chiefs	0–24	3–2
L	@ New York Jets	17–26	3–3
W	Denver Broncos	24–21	4–3
L	@ Boston Patriots	0–24	4–4
T	Cincinnati Bengals	31–31	4–4–1
T	@ Denver Broncos	20–20	4–4–2
W	@ Miami Dolphins	32–7	5–4–2
L	San Diego Chargers	17–21	5–5–2
L	New York Jets	26–34	5–6–2
W	Boston Patriots	27–23	6–6–2
L	*@ Oakland Raiders*	*7–56*	*0–1*

Season Leaders

CATEGORY	TOTAL	PLAYER
Passing Yards	2,455	Pete Beathard
Rushing Yards	740	Hoyle Granger
Receiving Yards	696	Jerry LeVias
Receptions	51	Alvin Reed
Interceptions	6	Miller Farr
Sacks	14.5	Elvin Bethea
Points	86	Roy Gerela

Key Additions:
Charlie Joiner (WR), Jerry LeVias (WR), Ron Pritchard (LB)

Starting Lineup

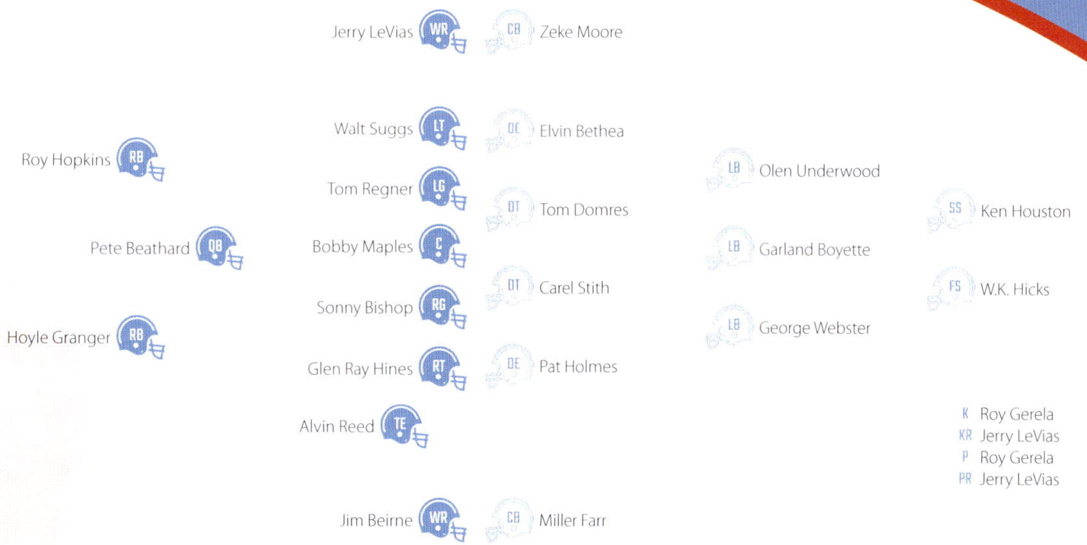

Offense		Defense	
WR	Jerry LeVias	CB	Zeke Moore
LT	Walt Suggs	DE	Elvin Bethea
LG	Tom Regner	DT	Tom Domres
C	Bobby Maples	DT	Carel Stith
RG	Sonny Bishop	DE	Pat Holmes
RT	Glen Ray Hines	LB	Olen Underwood
TE	Alvin Reed	LB	Garland Boyette
WR	Jim Beirne	LB	George Webster
QB	Pete Beathard	CB	Miller Farr
RB	Roy Hopkins	SS	Ken Houston
RB	Hoyle Granger	FS	W.K. Hicks

K Roy Gerela
KR Jerry LeVias
P Roy Gerela
PR Jerry LeVias

Titans Trivia

Elvin Bethea's 16 sacks in 1973 are the most in a single season by an Oilers/Titans player.

Pro Bowl Selections

- Jim Beirne (WR)
- Elvin Bethea (DE)
- Garland Boyette (LB)
- Miller Farr (CB)
- Glen Ray Hines (OT)
- Ken Houston (S)
- Jerry LeVias (WR)
- Zeke Moore (CB)
- Alvin Reed (TE)
- George Webster (LB)

All-1960s Offense

QUARTERBACK: George Blanda (1960–1966) served as the Houston Oilers' primary quarterback for the better part of seven seasons. Blanda spearheaded back-to-back AFL championship titles in 1960 and 1961. In 1961, he threw for league highs in passing yards (3,330) and touchdowns (36) en route to winning AFL Player of the Year. Blanda holds the Oilers/Titans all-time record for touchdown passes in a single season (36).

RUNNING BACKS: A Heisman Trophy winner out of LSU, Billy Cannon (1960–1963) led the Oilers in rushing as a rookie (644) and scored five receiving touchdowns. As a sophomore, Cannon led the AFL in rushing yards (948) and gained 1,534 all-purpose yards. Charley Tolar (1960–1966) became the first Oiler to surpass 1,000 rushing yards in a single season (1962). Tolar was named to two straight AFL All-Star teams (1961–1962).

WIDE RECEIVERS: Charley Hennigan (1960–1966) was a five-time AFL All-Star and two-time AFL leader in receiving yards. Hennigan currently ranks fourth all-time in franchise receiving yards (6,823). His 1,746 receiving yards in 1961 sit atop the Oilers/Titans all-time single-season leader board. In 1960, Bill Groman (1960–1962) became the first Oilers receiver to surpass 1,000 receiving yards (1,473), setting the single-season record among all rookies, which stood for more than 60 years. Groman amassed nearly 3,000 receiving yards during his three seasons in Houston.

TIGHT END: Bob McLeod (1961–1966) started 54 games and made 84 total appearances for the Oilers. His biggest impact came across the 1962 and 1963 seasons, accounting for 1,108 receiving yards and 11 touchdowns.

CENTER: Bob Schmidt (1961–1963) was the Oilers' center for three seasons. He started 40 straight games for a hard-nosed offensive line and was named to the AFL All-Star team during all three seasons in Houston.

GUARDS: Regarded as one of the most dominant blockers of his era, Bob Talamini (1960–1967) was crucial to the success of the early 1960s Oilers offense. He was selected to six AFL All-Star Games. Sonny Bishop (1964–1969) started 78 games for the Oilers and was named to the AFL All-Star team in 1968.

TACKLES: An aggressive demeanor earned Al Jamison (1960–1962) the nickname "Al the Assassin" during his playing days. Jamison helped the franchise win back-to-back AFL championships in 1960 and 1961. Walt Suggs (1961–1971) played in 137 consecutive games and even joined the Oilers in the NFL for two seasons following the AFL-NFL merger. Suggs was named to the AFL All-Star team in 1967 and 1968.

KICKER: George Blanda (1960–1966) doubled as the team's placekicker. He ranks fifth all-time in franchise history with 91 career field goals. His 301 extra points and 598 total points both rank third. Blanda was inducted into the Oilers/Titans Hall of Fame in 1999.

KICK RETURNER: Bobby Jancik (1962–1967) became the first Oiler to account for more than 1,000 kick-return yards in a single season when he totaled 1,317 in 1963. Jancik's 4,185 total kickoff-return yards still rank as the most in franchise history.

Statistics for the all-decade team are for the given decade only, unless otherwise noted.

All-1960s Defense

DEFENSIVE ENDS: Don Floyd (1960–1967) was an original Oiler and led the team in sacks twice (1960, 1964). Across eight seasons, he totaled 20.5 sacks. Floyd was a three-time AFL All-Star and was First-Team All-Pro in 1962. Gary Cutsinger (1962–1968) spent his entire career with the franchise. He led the Oilers in sacks in 1963, 1965, and 1966. He finished his career with 23.5 total sacks.

DEFENSIVE TACKLES: Ed Husmann (1961–1965) was one of the most dominant defenders in Oilers history. After signing as a free agent ahead of the 1961 season, he led the AFL with eight sacks. In 1962, he became the first player in franchise history to record 10-plus sacks in a season (10), once again leading the AFL in sacks. Pat Holmes (1966–1972) was a back-to-back AFL All-Star in 1967 and 1968. He was a key member of the 1967 squad that advanced to the AFL Championship Game.

LINEBACKERS: The Oilers selected George Webster (1967–1972) with the fifth overall pick in the 1967 AFL Draft. Webster made three consecutive AFL All-Star appearances in the decade. He is a member of the AFL All-Time Team. Doug Cline (1960–1966) made 93 appearances for the Oilers through seven seasons with the club. He recorded seven career interceptions and had one in the 1961 AFL Championship Game. Mike Dukes (1960–1963) played four seasons in Houston and was a ball magnet, totaling six interceptions with the team.

CORNERBACKS: Tony Banfield (1960–1963, 1965) tallied 27 career interceptions, which is tied for fourth all-time among Oilers/Titans defenders. Miller Farr (1967–1969) made a lasting impact in three seasons with the team. He was an AFL All-Star every year, and his 10 interceptions in 1967 rank third all-time in franchise history.

SAFETIES: Jim Norton (1960–1968) is the all-time interceptions leader in franchise history with 45. He was inducted into the Oilers/Titans Hall of Fame in 1999, and his legendary number 43 jersey was retired by the organization. Fred Glick (1961–1966) led the Oilers in interceptions twice. His league-leading 12 interceptions in 1963 are still tied for the most in a single season by an Oilers/Titans player.

PUNTER: The versatile Jim Norton (1960–1968) doubled as a punter. He punted on 522 occasions with an impressive average of 42.1 yards per punt.

PUNT RETURNER: Bobby Jancik (1962–1967) was the team's primary punt returner for the majority of his six-year stint in Houston. Jancik returned a punt for a touchdown in 1964 and averaged an eye-popping 18.3 yards per return that season. He averaged 9.7 yards per punt return during his career.

Charley Hennigan was First-Team All-Pro in 1961, 1962, and 1964.

1970

3–10–1
Fourth in AFC Central

The 1970 Oilers campaign was their first in the National Football League (NFL), following the AFL-NFL merger. The Oilers were placed in the AFC Central Division, joining the Cincinnati Bengals, Cleveland Browns, and Pittsburgh Steelers. The Oilers did not renew the contract of general manager Don Klosterman. He was replaced by Bob Brodhead, former quarterback for the Buffalo Bills.

Long-time right guard Sonny Bishop retired after the 1969 season and was replaced by Elbert Drungo. Defensive back W.K. Hicks was traded to the New York Jets for a fifth-round pick. The Oilers acquired quarterback Charley Johnson and defensive back Bob Atkins in a blockbuster trade with the Saint Louis Cardinals that sent them quarterback Pete Beathard and cornerback Miller Farr.

The personnel changes didn't help. Houston fielded a pitiful product in 1970. Johnson was largely ineffective. He threw for more interceptions (12) than touchdowns (7) and completed just 51.2% of his passes. He played in 10 games before his season was shortened by injury.

The offense scored a meager 15.5 points per contest, which ranked 20th out of 26 teams. The defense was even worse, giving up 25.1 points per game—second-most in the league.

A seven-game winless streak doomed the Oilers' season. They snapped the 0–6–1 stretch with a dominant win over the Denver Broncos. Jerry LeVias caught two touchdown passes in the first quarter, and the Oilers led 31–0 after three quarters. Denver scored three meaningless touchdowns in the fourth to make the final score respectable, 31–21.

The Oilers finished with a record of 3–10–1. Head coach Wally Lemm announced his plans to retire at the conclusion of the disappointing season.

Schedule

OPPONENT	SCORE	RECORD
@ Pittsburgh Steelers	19–7	1–0
Miami Dolphins	10–20	1–1
@ Cincinnati Bengals	20–13	2–1
Baltimore Colts	20–24	2–2
Pittsburgh Steelers	3–7	2–3
@ San Diego Chargers	31–31	2–3–1
@ Saint Louis Cardinals	0–44	2–4–1
@ Kansas City Chiefs	9–24	2–5–1
San Francisco 49ers	20–30	2–6–1
@ Cleveland Browns	14–28	2–7–1
Denver Broncos	31–21	3–7–1
Cleveland Browns	10–21	3–8–1
Cincinnati Bengals	20–30	3–9–1
@ Dallas Cowboys	10–52	3–10–1

Season Leaders

CATEGORY	TOTAL	PLAYER
Passing Yards	1,652	Charley Johnson
Rushing Yards	517	Joe Dawkins
Receiving Yards	604	Alvin Reed
Receptions	47	Alvin Reed
Interceptions	6	Zeke Moore
Sacks	10.5	Elvin Bethea
Points	77	Roy Gerela

Pro Bowl Selections

- Ken Houston (S)
- Zeke Moore (CB)

Key Additions:
Charley Johnson (QB)

Starting Lineup

OFFENSE	POSITION
Charley Johnson	QB
Mike Richardson	RB
Joe Dawkins	RB
Jerry LeVias	WR
Charlie Joiner	WR
Alvin Reed	TE
Walt Suggs	LT
Ken Gray	LG
Bobby Maples	C
Elbert Drungo	RG
Glen Ray Hines	RT

DEFENSE	POSITION
Pat Holmes	DE
Willie Parker	DT
Tom Domres	DT
Elvin Bethea	DE
Olen Underwood	OLB
Garland Boyette	MLB
Ron Pritchard	OLB
Leroy Mitchell	CB
Zeke Moore	CB
Ken Houston	SS
Johnny Peacock	FS

SPECIAL TEAMS	POSITION
Roy Gerela	K
Jerry LeVias	KR
Spike Jones	P
Jerry LeVias	PR

Zeke Moore (22) was an All-Star/Pro Bowl cornerback in 1969 and 1970.

1971

4-9-1
Third in AFC Central

The offseason before the 1971 campaign was filled with significant changes. Owner Bud Adams hired John Breen as the general manager. Ed Hughes was named head coach to replace recently retired Wally Lemm. Hughes had played professionally for the Los Angeles Rams and New York Giants, and he brought experience as a defensive backs coach.

Perhaps more notable than all the front-office turnover was the decision to draft quarterback Dan Pastorini with the third selection in the 1971 NFL Draft. Pastorini was the third quarterback drafted, after the New England Patriots picked Jim Plunkett and the New Orleans Saints took Archie Manning. (The Oilers actually doubled down at quarterback by drafting Lynn Dickey in the third round.)

A blockbuster trade saw the Oilers send running back Hoyle Granger, offensive tackle Terry Stoepel, and defensive end Charles Blossom to the New Orleans Saints for wide receiver Ken Burrough and defensive tackle Dave Rowe. Burrough's impact in the 1971 season was minor, but he would eventually find his rhythm with the team and become one of the franchise's all-time greats.

Pastorini made his first career start in Week 5, a 31–7 loss to the Detroit Lions. The rookie would eventually develop into a long-term solution at quarterback, but his first campaign was bumpy. Pastorini threw just seven touchdowns versus 21 interceptions.

Superstar safety Ken Houston made history by returning four interceptions for touchdowns. He also returned a fumble for a score.

The season began with a six-game winless streak. However, the Oilers concluded 1971 with three straight victories, providing hope for the future of the team.

Pro Bowl Selections

- Elvin Bethea (DE)
- Ken Houston (S)

Schedule

	OPPONENT	SCORE	RECORD
L	@ Cleveland Browns	0–31	0–1
L	Kansas City Chiefs	16–20	0–2
T	New Orleans Saints	13–13	0–2–1
L	@ Washington	13–22	0–3–1
L	Detroit Lions	7–31	0–4–1
L	@ Pittsburgh Steelers	16–23	0–5–1
W	Cincinnati Bengals	10–6	1–5–1
L	@ New England Patriots	20–28	1–6–1
L	@ Oakland Raiders	21–41	1–7–1
L	@ Cincinnati Bengals	13–28	1–8–1
L	Cleveland Browns	24–37	1–9–1
W	Pittsburgh Steelers	29–3	2–9–1
W	@ Buffalo Bills	20–14	3–9 –1
W	San Diego Chargers	49–33	4–9–1

Season Leaders

CATEGORY	TOTAL	PLAYER
Passing Yards	1,702	Dan Pastorini
Rushing Yards	288	Robert Holmes
Receiving Yards	681	Charlie Joiner
Receptions	38	Jim Beirne
Interceptions	9	Ken Houston
Sacks	10.5	Elvin Bethea
Points	73	Mark Moseley

Key Additions:
Willie Alexander (CB), Ken Burrough (WR), Dan Pastorini (QB), Mike Tilleman (DT)

Starting Lineup

OFFENSE	POSITION
Dan Pastorini	QB
Woody Campbell	RB
Robert Holmes	RB
Jim Beirne	WR
Charlie Joiner	WR
Alvin Reed	TE
Gene Ferguson	LT
Bob Young	LG
Walt Suggs	C
Elbert Drungo	RG
Sam Walton	RT

DEFENSE	POSITION
Pat Holmes	DE
Mike Tilleman	DT
Ron Billingsley	DT
Elvin Bethea	DE
George Webster	OLB
Garland Boyette	MLB
Ron Pritchard	OLB
Zeke Moore	CB
Willie Alexander	CB
Ken Houston	SS
John Charles	FS

SPECIAL TEAMS	POSITION
Mark Moseley	K
Linzy Cole	KR
Dan Pastorini	P
Ken Houston	PR

Willie Alexander started 98 games in his career and intercepted 23 passes.

1972

1–13
Fourth in AFC Central

Ed Hughes did not return as the head coach after a 4–9–1 season in 1971. Hughes was replaced by Bill Peterson, who was previously a head coach in college at Florida State and Rice University. It was Peterson's first (and only) opportunity to lead a professional franchise.

The 1972 Oilers were miserable. They finished with a league-worst 1–13 record. Coach Peterson fielded the most inept offense in franchise history. Throughout the course of the 14-game schedule, the Oilers scored a franchise-low 11.7 points per contest. They were shut out on two occasions, once by the Oakland Raiders, 34–0, on Monday Night Football, and later in the season by the Cleveland Browns, 20–0. The painful prime-time defeat to the Raiders saw Houston finish that game with an astonishing -1 net passing yards.

Coincidentally, the lone win had come one week earlier. After falling behind the New York Jets, 10–0, the Oilers put two touchdowns on the board in the second quarter, including a 52-yard connection from quarterback Dan Pastorini to wide receiver Ken Burrough. Powered by Skip Butler's four second-half field goals, Houston held on to win, 26–20.

The Oilers concluded the forgettable season with another franchise-low moment. They were handily defeated, 61–17, by the Cincinnati Bengals, putting an appropriate bow on a nightmare campaign.

Adding insult to injury, a critical error was made mid-season. The Oilers traded wide receiver Charlie Joiner and linebacker Ron Pritchard to the Cincinnati Bengals in exchange for running backs Fred Willis and Paul Robinson. Joiner never reached his performance ceiling with the Oilers, but he became a superstar with the San Diego Chargers. Joiner was inducted into the Pro Football Hall of Fame in 1996. The Oilers let an all-time great get away.

Houston debuted a new look in 1972. Their helmets had been light blue from 1960 to 1965. Silver was the main color from 1966 to 1971. In 1972, the team went back to light-blue helmets that matched their home jerseys and—for the first time ever—light-blue pants worn on the road.

Schedule

OPPONENT	SCORE	RECORD
@ Denver Broncos	17–30	0–1
@ Miami Dolphins	13–34	0–2
New York Jets	26–20	1–2
Oakland Raiders	0–34	1–3
@ Pittsburgh Steelers	7–24	1–4
Cleveland Browns	17–23	1–5
@ Cincinnati Bengals	7–30	1–6
@ Cleveland Browns	0–20	1–7
Philadelphia Eagles	17–18	1–8
Green Bay Packers	10–23	1–9
@ San Diego Chargers	20–34	1–10
@ Atlanta Falcons	10–20	1–11
Pittsburgh Steelers	3–9	1–12
Cincinnati Bengals	17–61	1–13

Season Leaders

CATEGORY	TOTAL	PLAYER
Passing Yards	1,711	Dan Pastorini
Rushing Yards	355	Paul Robinson
Receiving Yards	521	Ken Burrough
Receptions	36	Fred Willis
Interceptions	2	B. Atkins, J. Charles
Sacks	11	Mike Tilleman
Points	51	Skip Butler

Key Additions:
Skip Butler (K), Greg Sampson (DT), Fred Willis (RB)

Starting Lineup

Titans Trivia

Oilers defensive tackle Mike Tilleman finished tied for fourth in the league with 11 sacks.

Pro Bowl Selections

- Elvin Bethea (DE)
- Ken Houston (S)

29
41

Houston, We Have a Problem

Sandwiched between the two worst seasons in Oilers history, new general manager Sid Gillman decided the roster was in need of a major shake-up ahead of the 1973 season. The most notable move arrived when Gillman traded Pro Bowl safety Ken Houston to Washington in exchange for tight end Mack Alston, defensive end Mike Fanucci, wide receiver Clifton McNeil, defensive back Jeff Severson, and offensive lineman Jim Snowden. It is remembered as one of the worst trades in NFL history.

Ken Houston had been a top performer for the Oilers since getting drafted in the ninth round of the 1967 NFL/AFL Draft. He recorded four interceptions as a rookie and helped his team reach the AFL Championship Game. In the five seasons that followed, Houston intercepted 21 passes, recovered 10 fumbles, scored eight defensive touchdowns, and was named to the All-Star/Pro Bowl team every year.

In Washington, Houston only got better. He played for another eight years. He was chosen for seven consecutive Pro Bowls and was First-Team All-Pro twice.

As for the Oilers' end of the trade, Alston turned out to be the most productive player. In four seasons with the club, he started 47 games and gained 783 yards receiving. Severson started 18 games in two seasons with the Oilers. Fanucci was with the team for one season and never started a game. McNeil saw action in just three games. Snowden never played for the Oilers.

Ken Houston (29) was named to 12-straight All-Star/Pro Bowl teams in his 14-year career.

1973

1–13

Fourth in AFC Central

The offseason heading into 1973 was significant. General manager John Breen was replaced by Sid Gillman, a legendary coach-turned-executive who had enjoyed a successful stint with the San Diego Chargers. Notable personnel moves would follow. Most surprisingly, star safety Ken Houston was traded to Washington in exchange for five veteran players. (See page 41.)

Other changes included the departures of tight end Alvin Reed, defensive end Pat Holmes, and defensive tackle Mike Tilleman. Tilleman was traded to the Atlanta Falcons in exchange for a first-round pick, which the Oilers used on running back George Amundson. He only lasted two seasons with the team.

Houston's other first-round pick was spent on defensive lineman John Matuszak. He made a solid impression on the field after racking up four sacks, and he became infamous for his controversial lifestyle off the field. Matuszak lasted just one season in Houston. The franchise traded him for a future hall-of-famer. (See page 44.)

Overall, the 1973 season was as miserable as the previous one. Head coach Bill Peterson was dismissed following an abysmal 0–5 start. His 1–18 record across one-and-a-half seasons set an all-time franchise mark for worst winning percentage: .053. Peterson was replaced by Gillman, who added head coaching duties to his workload as general manager and executive vice president.

The Oilers finished with a league-worst 1–13 record for a second straight season. They were awful on offense and defense, leading to a historically poor point differential of -248. The defense allowed a league-worst 31.9 points per contest.

Starting quarterback Dan Pastorini was outperformed by his backup, Lynn Dickey, who threw more touchdowns (six) in four starts than Pastorini managed in 10 starts (five). Houston's only win came with Dickey under center. He threw for 340 yards and three touchdowns to lift the Oilers, 31–27, in Baltimore. Pro Bowl defensive end Elvin Bethea was the season's only shining star. He set an unofficial franchise record with 16 sacks in 1973.

Schedule

	OPPONENT	SCORE	RECORD
L	@ New York Giants	14–34	0–1
L	@ Cincinnati Bengals	10–24	0–2
L	Pittsburgh Steelers	7–36	0–3
L	Los Angeles Rams	26–31	0–4
L	Denver Broncos	20–48	0–5
L	@ Cleveland Browns	13–42	0–6
L	@ Chicago Bears	14–35	0–7
W	@ Baltimore Colts	31–27	1–7
L	Cleveland Browns	13–23	1–8
L	@ Kansas City Chiefs	14–38	1–9
L	New England Patriots	0–32	1–10
L	Oakland Raiders	6–17	1–11
L	@ Pittsburgh Steelers	7–33	1–12
L	Cincinnati Bengals	24–27	1–13

Season Leaders

CATEGORY	TOTAL	PLAYER
Passing Yards	1,482	Dan Pastorini
Rushing Yards	579	Fred Willis
Receiving Yards	581	Billy Parks
Receptions	57	Fred Willis
Interceptions	4	G. Roberts, J. Severson
Sacks	16	Elvin Bethea
Points	66	Skip Butler

Key Additions:
Gregg Bingham (LB), Tody Smith (DE), Ted Washington (LB)

Starting Lineup

Titans Trivia

The 1973 season marks the only time in franchise history the Oilers/Titans didn't capture a single home victory.

Pro Bowl Selections

- Elvin Bethea (DE)

1974

7–7
Second in AFC Central

Sid Gillman returned as the Oilers head coach for the 1974 season. He put together an impressive coaching staff that included defensive assistant Ed Biles, who had previously spent time with the New York Jets and New Orleans Saints. Gillman named O.A. "Bum" Phillips as the defensive coordinator. Phillips is considered a founding father of the 3-4 defense, which the Oilers began utilizing upon his arrival in 1974.

In late October, Gillman executed a blockbuster trade. The Oilers acquired defensive tackle Curley Culp and a first-round pick in the 1975 NFL Draft from the Kansas City Chiefs in exchange for John Matuszak, who had threatened to jump to a rival football league and was involved in a legal-related standoff with the Oilers. It would go down as one of the greatest trades in franchise history.

Another notable acquisition was the draft selection of wide receiver and special teams ace Billy "White Shoes" Johnson in the 15th round of the 1974 NFL Draft. Johnson quickly became a fan favorite, with his quickness serving as a threat in the open field.

Change led to a much-improved team. A midseason four-game winning streak was highlighted by a seesaw affair against the New Your Jets. A Zeke Moore pick-six and a 29-yard touchdown connection from Dan Pastorini to Johnson helped the Oilers jump ahead, 14–6. But the lead changed three times in the second half. Trailing 22–20 in the fourth, Houston won the game on a one-yard touchdown plunge by running back Willie Rodgers.

The winning streak helped the Oilers finish with a respectable 7–7 record, although they missed the postseason for a fifth consecutive time. Houston's seven victories were more than the previous three seasons combined. The 1974 campaign turned around the franchise's fortunes. Better results were on the horizon.

Pro Bowl Selections

- Elvin Bethea (DE)

Schedule

	OPPONENT	SCORE	RECORD
W	San Diego Chargers	21–14	1–0
L	@ Cleveland Browns	7–20	1–1
L	Kansas City Chiefs	7–17	1–2
L	Pittsburgh Steelers	7–13	1–3
L	@ Minnesota Vikings	10–51	1–4
L	Saint Louis Cardinals	27–31	1–5
W	@ Cincinnati Bengals	34–21	2–5
W	@ New York Jets	27–22	3–5
W	@ Buffalo Bills	21–9	4–5
W	Cincinnati Bengals	20–3	5–5
L	Dallas Cowboys	0–10	5–6
W	@ Pittsburgh Steelers	13–10	6–6
L	@ Denver Broncos	14–37	6–7
W	Cleveland Browns	28–24	7–7

Season Leaders

CATEGORY	TOTAL	PLAYER
Passing Yards	1,571	Dan Pastorini
Rushing Yards	413	Willie Rodgers
Receiving Yards	492	Ken Burrough
Receptions	36	Ken Burrough
Interceptions	6	Bob Atkins
Sacks	11	Ted Washington
Points	56	Skip Butler

Key Additions:
Ronnie Coleman (RB), Curley Culp (DT), Ed Fisher (G), Billy Johnson (WR), Steve Kiner (LB)

Starting Lineup

OFFENSE	POSITION
Dan Pastorini	QB
Vic Washington	RB
Willie Rodgers	RB
Ken Burrough	WR
Billy Parks	WR
Mack Alston	TE
Greg Sampson	LT
Harris Jones	LG
Sid Smith	C
Brian Goodman	RG
Elbert Drungo	RT

DEFENSE	POSITION
Tody Smith	DE
Curley Culp	NT
Elvin Bethea	DE
Al Cowlings	OLB
Gregg Bingham	ILB
Steve Kiner	ILB
Ted Washington	OLB
Willie Alexander	CB
Zeke Moore	CB
Al Johnson	SS
Bob Atkins	FS

SPECIAL TEAMS	POSITION
Skip Butler	K
Billy Johnson	KR
David Beverly	P
Billy Johnson	PR

"Attitude is the whole thing in football. Every team has the talent and the coaching. Motivation makes the difference."

—Sid Gillman

After playing in just one game in 1973, Ted Washington became a full-time starter in 1974.

1975

10–4
Third in AFC Central

In late January, general manager Sid Gillman named defensive coordinator O.A. "Bum" Phillips the new head coach. The franchise and Gillman parted ways just weeks later. Phillips, like Gillman, would pull double-duty as GM and head coach. Defensive assistant Ed Biles was promoted to defensive coordinator, and former NFL quarterback King Hill was named the offensive coordinator.

The Oilers enjoyed success under Phillips' innovative direction. The stingy defense allowed just 16.1 points per game, fifth-best in the league. The Oilers finished the season 10–4, clinching their first winning record since 1967 and their best overall season since 1962.

Unfortunately, all four of their losses came against their division rivals the Pittsburgh Steelers and Cincinnati Bengals. As a result, the Steelers won the division, and the Bengals claimed the lone wild-card spot. The Oilers missed the playoffs for a sixth consecutive season.

Defensive tackle Curley Culp recorded a career-high 11.5 sacks and was in the running for the NFL Defensive Player of the Year. The dominant duo of Culp and Elvin Bethea combined for 21.5 sacks, and rookie pass-rusher Robert Brazile contributed an additional seven sacks. Brazile was named Defensive Rookie of the Year.

The Oilers had drafted Brazile with a pick they acquired from the Kansas City Chiefs—a deal that also included Curley Culp—in exchange for John Matuszak. Houston gained two future hall-of-famers in one trade.

Billy "White Shoes" Johnson established himself as one of the league's elite special-teams returners. Johnson tied an NFL record with four touchdown returns (three punts, one kickoff) in one season.

Schedule

	OPPONENT	SCORE	RECORD
W	@ New England Patriots	7–0	1–0
W	San Diego Chargers	33–17	2–0
L	Cincinnati Bengals	19–21	2–1
W	@ Cleveland Browns	40–10	3–1
W	Washington	13–10	4–1
W	Detroit Lions	24–8	5–1
W	@ Kansas City Chiefs	17–13	6–1
L	@ Pittsburgh Steelers	17–24	6–2
W	Miami Dolphins	20–19	7–2
L	Pittsburgh Steelers	9–32	7–3
L	@ Cincinnati Bengals	19–23	7–4
W	@ San Francisco 49ers	27–13	8–4
W	@ Oakland Raiders	27–26	9–4
W	Cleveland Browns	21–10	10–4

Season Leaders

CATEGORY	TOTAL	PLAYER
Passing Yards	2,053	Dan Pastorini
Rushing Yards	790	Ronnie Coleman
Receiving Yards	1,063	Ken Burrough
Receptions	53	Ken Burrough
Interceptions	5	Zeke Moore
Sacks	11.5	Curley Culp
Points	85	Skip Butler

Pro Bowl Selections

- Elvin Bethea (DE)
- Ken Burrough (WR)
- Curley Culp (NT)
- Billy Johnson (KR)
- Dan Pastorini (QB)

Key Additions:
Robert Brazile (LB), Carl Mauck (C), Greg Stemrick (CB)

Curley Culp was inducted into the Pro Football Hall of Fame in 2013.

Starting Lineup

OFFENSE	POSITION
Dan Pastorini	QB
Ronnie Coleman	RB
Don Hardeman	RB
Ken Burrough	WR
Billy Johnson	WR
Mack Alston	TE
Greg Sampson	LT
Ron Saul	LG
Carl Mauck	C
Ed Fisher	RG
Elbert Drungo	RT

DEFENSE	POSITION
Tody Smith	DE
Curley Culp	NT
Elvin Bethea	DE
Ted Washington	OLB
Steve Kiner	MLB
Gregg Bingham	MLB
Robert Brazile	OLB
Willie Alexander	CB
Zeke Moore	CB
Willie Germany	SS
C.L. Whittington	FS

SPECIAL TEAMS	POSITION
Skip Butler	K
Billy Johnson	KR
Dan Pastorini	P
Billy Johnson	PR

1976

5–9

Fourth in AFC Central

Head coach Bum Phillips hired his son, Wade Phillips, as a defensive assistant ahead of the 1976 season. It represented Wade's first professional opportunity after coaching for three collegiate programs. Wade would eventually develop into a successful defensive coordinator and head coach.

In April, the Oilers traded backup quarterback Lynn Dickey to the Green Bay Packers in exchange for quarterback John Hadl, cornerback Ken Ellis, two draft picks, and cash considerations. Hadl ended up starting four games for the Oilers late in the season and struggled. Dickey would go on to have a solid career with the Packers.

Two games into the season, the Oilers made another trade. They acquired safety Mike Reinfeldt in a deal with the Oakland Raiders. Reinfeldt's impact was minimal in 1976, but he'd eventually develop into a key player (and a future front-office executive for the franchise).

The Oilers initially appeared capable of building upon the 10-win campaign of 1975. They jumped out to an impressive 4–1 record. That's when things fell apart. A six-game losing streak dropped the Oilers to a hapless 4–7.

A late-season victory over the Atlanta Falcons momentarily stopped the bleeding. Hadl connected on a 40-yard touchdown score to Billy Johnson in the third quarter, which gave Houston the lead and ultimately the victory, 20–14. Johnson finished with 104 receiving yards on the day. Nevertheless, the Oilers finished with a record of 5–9. They failed to qualify for the playoffs for a seventh consecutive season.

Elvin Bethea enjoyed a four-sack performance in a midseason loss to the San Diego Chargers. Bethea also recovered a fumble in that game. Although he totaled a team-high 14.5 sacks in 1976, he was not voted to the Pro Bowl.

Schedule

OPPONENT	SCORE	RECORD
Tampa Bay Buccaneers	20–0	1–0
@ Buffalo Bills	13–3	2–0
Oakland Raiders	13–14	2–1
@ New Orleans Saints	31–26	3–1
Denver Broncos	17–3	4–1
@ San Diego Chargers	27–30	4–2
Cincinnati Bengals	7–27	4–3
@ Baltimore Colts	14–38	4–4
Cleveland Browns	7–21	4–5
@ Cincinnati Bengals	27–31	4–6
@ Pittsburgh Steelers	16–32	4–7
Atlanta Falcons	20–14	5–7
@ Cleveland Browns	10–13	5–8
Pittsburgh Steelers	0–21	5–9

Season Leaders

CATEGORY	TOTAL	PLAYER
Passing Yards	1,795	Dan Pastorini
Rushing Yards	684	Ronnie Coleman
Receiving Yards	932	Ken Burrough
Receptions	51	Ken Burrough
Interceptions	5	C.L. Whittington
Sacks	14.5	Elvin Bethea
Points	72	Skip Butler

Pro Bowl Selections

- Robert Brazile (LB)
- Curley Culp (NT)

Key Additions:
Mike Barber (TE), Mike Reinfeldt (S)

Billy "White Shoes" Johnson scored eight career return touchdowns.

Starting Lineup

OFFENSE	POSITION
Dan Pastorini	QB
Ronnie Coleman	RB
Fred Willis	RB
Ken Burrough	WR
Billy Johnson	WR
Mack Alston	TE
Greg Sampson	LT
Conway Hayman	LG
Carl Mauck	C
Ed Fisher	RG
Elbert Drungo	RT

DEFENSE	POSITION
Tody Smith	DE
Curley Culp	NT
Elvin Bethea	DE
Ted Washington	OLB
Steve Kiner	ILB
Gregg Bingham	ILB
Robert Brazile	OLB
Willie Alexander	CB
Zeke Moore	CB
Mike Reinfeldt	SS
C.L. Whittington	FS

SPECIAL TEAMS	POSITION
Skip Butler	K
Billy Johnson	KR
Dan Pastorini	P
Billy Johnson	PR

1977

8–6
Third in AFC Central

Bum Phillips made a notable coaching staff change ahead of the season. Offensive coordinator King Hill was downgraded to wide receivers coach. Former New Orleans Saints, New York Jets, and Detroit Lions offensive coordinator Ken Shipp assumed Hill's previous role.

The Oilers began the season with an impressive 3–1 record. Phillips' stingy defense held three of the first four opponents to 10 points or fewer. But then unfortunate injuries began derailing a promising season.

Starting quarterback Dan Pastorini suffered ankle and back injuries in a victory over the Pittsburgh Steelers. He was in and out of the lineup for the next few games. Superstar pass rusher Elvin Bethea suffered a broken arm in a mid-November loss to the Oakland Raiders. Prior to the injury, Bethea was on an iron-man streak, having appeared in 135 straight contests.

The Oilers remained inconsistent for the remainder of the season. Despite a 4–1 record to end the campaign, in the ultra-competitive AFC Central, the 8–6 Oilers finished third in the division behind the Steelers (9–5) and the Cincinnati Bengals (8–6), who held the tiebreaker over the Oilers.

Houston's offense scored a fifth-ranked 21.4 points per contest. The Oilers scored 27-plus points on four occasions, including a memorable 47–0 win over the Chicago Bears. Electric returner Billy "White Shoes" Johnson scored three return touchdowns during the 1977 season, in addition to three receiving touchdowns. He was First-Team All-Pro.

Although the Oilers missed the playoffs for an eighth straight season, the team was trending in the right direction. Positive changes were on the horizon, which began with a home-run selection in the 1978 NFL Draft.

Pro Bowl Selections

- Robert Brazile (LB)
- Ken Burrough (WR)
- Curley Culp (NT)
- Billy Johnson (KR)

Schedule

	OPPONENT	SCORE	RECORD
W	New York Jets	20–0	1–0
W	@ Green Bay Packers	16–10	2–0
L	@ Miami Dolphins	7–27	2–1
W	Pittsburgh Steelers	27–10	3–1
L	Cleveland Browns	23–24	3–2
L	@ Pittsburgh Steelers	10–27	3–3
L	@ Cincinnati Bengals (OT)	10–13	3–4
W	Chicago Bears	47–0	4–4
L	@ Oakland Raiders	29–34	4–5
W	@ Seattle Seahawks	22–10	5–5
W	Kansas City Chiefs	34–20	6–5
L	Denver Broncos	14–24	6–6
W	@ Cleveland Browns	19–15	7–6
W	Cincinnati Bengals	21–16	8–6

Season Leaders

CATEGORY	TOTAL	PLAYER
Passing Yards	1,987	Dan Pastorini
Rushing Yards	660	Ronnie Coleman
Receiving Yards	816	Ken Burrough
Receptions	43	Ken Burrough
Interceptions	5	Mike Reinfeldt
Sacks	7.5	Jim Young
Points	55	Toni Fritsch

Key Additions:
Toni Fritsch (K), Cliff Parsley (P)

Starting Lineup

OFFENSE	POSITION
Dan Pastorini	QB
Ronnie Coleman	RB
Tim Wilson	RB
Ken Burrough	WR
Eddie Foster	WR
Mike Barber	TE
Greg Sampson	LT
George Reihner	LG
Carl Mauck	C
Elbert Drungo	RG
Kevin Hunt	RT

DEFENSE	POSITION
Jim Young	DE
Curley Culp	NT
Elvin Bethea	DE
Ted Washington	OLB
Steve Kiner	ILB
Gregg Bingham	ILB
Robert Brazile	OLB
Willie Alexander	CB
Zeke Moore	CB
Bill Currier	SS
Mike Reinfeldt	FS

SPECIAL TEAMS	POSITION
Toni Fritsch	K
Billy Johnson	KR
Cliff Parsley	P
Billy Johnson	PR

"Two kinds of ballplayers aren't worth a darn: one that never does what he's told and one who does nothin' except what he's told."

—Bum Phillips

Ken Burrough was named to his second and final Pro Bowl in 1977.

1978

10–6
Second in AFC Central

The NFL shifted to a 16-game schedule ahead of the 1978 season. The Houston Oilers acquired the top overall pick in the 1978 NFL Draft from the Tampa Bay Buccaneers in exchange for the 17th and 44th picks, as well as third- and fifth-round picks in 1979, and tight end Jimmie Giles. Oilers general manager and head coach Bum Phillips chose running back Earl Campbell, the reigning Heisman Trophy winner from the University of Texas.

Campbell immediately repaid the Oilers on their investment. He rushed for a league-leading 1,450 yards en route to Offensive Rookie of the Year and AFC Offensive Player of the Year honors. He was also named the NFL's Most Valuable Player (MVP) by the Pro Football Writers of America (PFWA). Campbell's 1,450 rushing yards set an Oilers single-season record.

Four games into the season, quarterback Dan Pastorini and offensive coordinator Ken Shipp were involved in a shouting match over who deserved blame for a Week 4 loss to the Los Angeles Rams. Shipp publicly blamed Pastorini, who denied responsibility for a call that led to an interception. Phillips sided with Pastorini by relieving Shipp of his duties.

In Week 8, a 24–17 victory over the Pittsburgh Steelers qualified as Houston's first-ever win on Monday Night Football. Weeks later, the Oilers rallied from 23–0 to defeat the New England Patriots, 26–23. Yet Houston's most memorable regular-season victory came when the Oilers defeated the Miami Dolphins on Monday Night Football, 35–30, in an instant classic. Campbell rushed for 199 yards and four touchdowns, including a highlight-reel 81-yard score in the fourth quarter.

Many credit that victory as the unofficial beginning of Houston's infamous "Luv Ya Blue" era. Attending fans were given blue-and-white pom-poms, which they waved throughout the contest.

In the playoffs, with stellar games from Campbell and Pastorini, Houston handled the Dolphins and the New England Patriots on the road. They advanced to the AFC Championship Game for the first time in franchise history. The Steelers exacted their revenge by dominating the Oilers, 34–5. Poor weather conditions led to nine Oilers turnovers.

Schedule

	OPPONENT	SCORE	RECORD
L	@ Atlanta Falcons	14–20	0–1
W	@ Kansas City Chiefs	20–17	1–1
W	San Francisco 49ers	20–19	2–1
L	Los Angeles Rams	6–10	2–2
W	@ Cleveland Browns	16–13	3–2
L	@ Oakland Raiders	17–21	3–3
W	Buffalo Bills	17–10	4–3
W	@ Pittsburgh Steelers	24–17	5–3
L	@ Cincinnati Bengals	13–28	5–4
W	Cleveland Browns	14–10	6–4
W	@ New England Patriots	26–23	7–4
W	Miami Dolphins	35–30	8–4
W	Cincinnati Bengals	17–10	9–4
L	Pittsburgh Steelers	3–13	9–5
W	@ New Orleans Saints	17–12	10–5
L	San Diego Chargers	24–45	10–6
W	*@ Miami Dolphins*	*17–9*	*1–0*
W	*@ New England Patriots*	*31–14*	*2–0*
L	*@ Pittsburgh Steelers*	*5–34*	*2–1*

Season Leaders

CATEGORY	TOTAL	PLAYER
Passing Yards	2,473	Dan Pastorini
Rushing Yards	1,450	Earl Campbell
Receiving Yards	624	Ken Burrough
Receptions	47	Ken Burrough
Interceptions	5	Willie Alexander
Sacks	8	Elvin Bethea
Points	78	Earl Campbell

Key Additions:
Earl Campbell (RB), Mike Renfro (WR)

Starting Lineup

WR Ken Burrough
LT Greg Sampson
LG George Reihner
C Carl Mauck
RG Ed Fisher
RT Conway Hayman
TE Mike Barber
WR Mike Renfro
RB Earl Campbell
QB Dan Pastorini
RB Tim Wilson

CB Greg Stemrick
DE Elvin Bethea
NT Curley Culp
DE Jim Young
CB Willie Alexander
LB Robert Brazile
LB Gregg Bingham
LB Steve Kiner
LB Ted Washington
SS Bill Currier
FS Mike Reinfeldt

K Toni Fritsch
KR Johnnie Dirden
P Cliff Parsley
PR Ronnie Coleman

Titans Trivia

Linebacker Robert Brazile recorded a career-high 185 tackles during the 1978 campaign.

Pro Bowl Selections

- Elvin Bethea (DE)
- Robert Brazile (LB)
- Earl Campbell (RB)
- Curley Culp (NT)

The Tyler Rose

As a rookie, Earl Campbell rushed for a league-leading 1,450 yards and won the awards for Offensive Rookie of the Year and AFC Offensive Player of the Year. Campbell was also named the NFL's Most Valuable Player (MVP) by the Pro Football Writers of America.

As good as he was, Campbell was even better in 1979. The punishing runner galloped for a league-leading 1,697 yards and 19 touchdowns. He was crowned the league's rushing champion for a second consecutive season and became the first player in franchise history to be named the Associated Press's MVP.

His ascension continued in 1980. Campbell rushed for a career-high 1,934 yards, while averaging a personal-best 5.2 yards per carry. At the time, his 1,934 yards ranked second in NFL history (behind O.J. Simpson's 2,003 yards in 1973). Campbell won his third straight rushing title and a third straight NFL Offensive Player of the Year award.

The Oilers fired head coach Bum Phillips ahead of the 1981 season, a decision that impacted Campbell's effectiveness. The All-Pro running back rushed for 1,376 yards and 10 touchdowns, career lows in both categories. The team wasn't very good in the latter years of Campbell's tenure in Houston. They went 1–8 in the strike-shortened 1982 season, with Campbell rushing for just 538 yards. The Oilers traded Campbell to the New Orleans Saints midway through the 1984 season.

Campbell's run from 1978 through 1980 was legendary, marking one of the best three-year spans of any running back ever. He will forever be honored as an all-time franchise great.

Campbell was nicknamed the Tyler Rose for his hometown of Tyler, Texas.

34

1979

11–5

Second in AFC Central

By the 1979 season, "Luv Ya Blue" fever had completely taken over the fan base. The movement gave each game a college-like atmosphere—with everything from pom-poms to fight songs. The Oilers were again led by running back Earl Campbell, who somehow outdid his rookie performance. He rushed for a league-leading 1,697 yards and 19 touchdowns, and he became the first player in franchise history to be named the Associated Press's MVP.

Houston's defense was led by a revelation of its own. Second-round pick Jesse Baker burst onto the scene, recording a team-leading 15.5 sacks as a rookie. Baker, who was named to the NFL's All-Rookie Team, started just two games. Safety Mike Reinfeldt led the league in interceptions with 12, trying Fred Glick's single-season record from 1963.

The Oilers' 11 regular-season wins matched the franchise's season-best from 1962. They hosted their first playoff game since 1962, against the Denver Broncos. A pair of Toni Fritsch field goals, combined with a three-yard rushing touchdown by Campbell, gave the Oilers a 13–7 victory. Unfortunately, Campbell, starting quarterback Dan Pastorini, and team-leading wide receiver Ken Burrough were all injured in the win.

Thanks to their stellar defense, the Oilers overcame that adversity to outlast the San Diego Chargers, 17–14, in the divisional round of the playoffs. Safety Vernon Perry was the hero, intercepting Chargers quarterback Dan Fouts an NFL-playoff-record four times. Perry actually accounted for five takeaways, blocking a field goal that he returned into Chargers territory.

For the second consecutive AFC Championship Game, the Oilers faced their AFC Central rival Pittsburgh Steelers. Oilers wide receiver Mike Renfro was denied a game-tying touchdown. A leaping Renfro appeared to get both feet in bounds, but he was ruled out of bounds. It went down as one of the most controversial rulings in football history and was credited by some for the NFL's willingness to eventually adopt an instant replay system. The back-and-forth battle was a one-score game until late in the fourth quarter, when a four-yard touchdown run by Rocky Bleier sealed the win for Pittsburgh, 27–13.

Schedule

	OPPONENT	SCORE	RECORD
W	@ Washington	29–27	1–0
L	@ Pittsburgh Steelers	7–38	1–1
W	Kansas City Chiefs	20–6	2–1
W	@ Cincinnati Bengals (OT)	30–27	3–1
W	Cleveland Browns	31–10	4–1
L	Saint Louis Cardinals	17–24	4–2
W	@ Baltimore Colts	28–16	5–2
L	@ Seattle Seahawks	14–34	5–3
W	New York Jets (OT)	27–24	6–3
W	@ Miami Dolphins	9–6	7–3
W	Oakland Raiders	31–17	8–3
W	Cincinnati Bengals	42–21	9–3
W	@ Dallas Cowboys	30–24	10–3
L	@ Cleveland Browns	7–14	10–4
W	Pittsburgh Steelers	20–17	11–4
L	Philadelphia Eagles	20–26	11–5
W	*Denver Broncos*	*13–7*	*1–0*
W	*@ San Diego Chargers*	*17–14*	*2–0*
L	*@ Pittsburgh Steelers*	*13–27*	*2–1*

Season Leaders

CATEGORY	TOTAL	PLAYER
Passing Yards	2,090	Dan Pastorini
Rushing Yards	1,697	Earl Campbell
Receiving Yards	752	Ken Burrough
Receptions	40	Ken Burrough
Interceptions	12	Mike Reinfeldt
Sacks	15.5	Jesse Baker
Points	114	Earl Campbell

Key Additions:
Jesse Baker (DE), Leon Gray (OT), Vernon Perry (S), Mike Stensrud (DL)

Starting Lineup

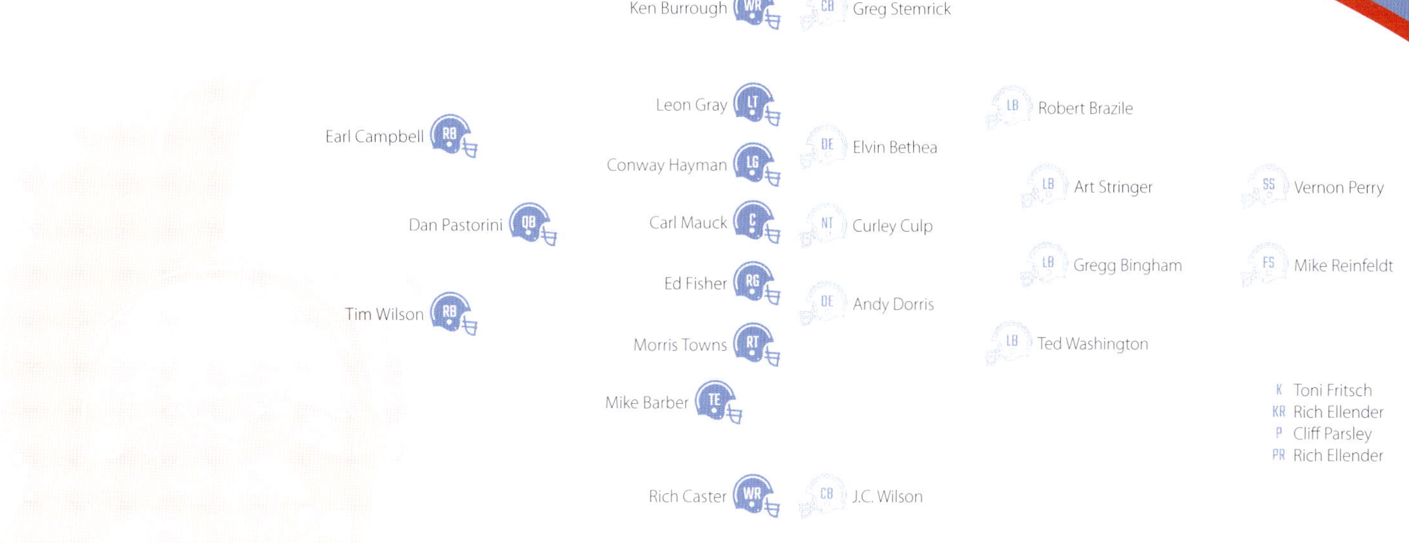

Titans Trivia

Reserve linebacker Ted Thompson went on to become a front-office executive, winning a Super Bowl with the Green Bay Packers.

Pro Bowl Selections

- Elvin Bethea (DE)
- Robert Brazile (LB)
- Earl Campbell (RB)
- Toni Fritsch (K)
- Leon Gray (OT)
- Mike Reinfeldt (S)

All-1970s Offense

QUARTERBACK: Dan Pastorini (1971–1979) struggled in his first few seasons, but he hit his stride toward the conclusion of the decade. Pastorini led the Oilers to back-to-back AFC Championship appearances in 1978 and 1979. He ranks fourth all-time in Oilers/Titans passing yards (16,864), fourth in touchdowns (96), and third in wins (53).

RUNNING BACKS: Earl Campbell (1978–1984) rushed for more than 3,000 yards and 32 touchdowns in just two seasons of the decade. He won the league's MVP in 1979 and is one of the greatest Oilers in history. Prior to Campbell's arrival, no Oiler had rushed for more than 790 yards in a single season throughout the decade. Ronnie Coleman (1974–1981) led the Oilers in rushing for three consecutive seasons prior to Campbell's arrival and ran for 2,596 yards in the 1970s. He added 860 receiving yards.

WIDE RECEIVERS: Ken Burrough (1971–1981) led the team in receiving yards seven times. He was the NFL's lone receiver to top 1,000 yards in 1975 and was named to two Pro Bowls. Burrough ranks third in franchise history with 6,906 receiving yards and is tied for second in receiving touchdowns with 47. Billy "White Shoes" Johnson (1974–1980) made touchdown celebrations popular with his rendition of the "Funky Chicken." He electrified crowds with his breathtaking speed. He gained 1,806 receiving yards and scored 13 offensive touchdowns.

TIGHT END: Alvin Reed (1967–1972) only spent three seasons with the Oilers during the 1970s, but he was the team's most productive tight end. Reed accounted for 1,263 receiving yards and three touchdowns. Mike Barber and Mack Alston also garnered consideration.

CENTER: A model of consistency, Carl Mauck (1975–1981) started 74 consecutive regular-season contests from 1975 to 1979—every Oilers game across those five seasons.

GUARDS: Elbert Drungo (1969–1977) was a versatile offensive lineman who started at guard and tackle. He was the starting right guard in 1970, 1971, and again in 1977. Ed Fisher (1974–1982) was the right guard for both squads that reached the AFC Championship Game. He started 60 games throughout the decade.

TACKLES: Greg Sampson (1972–1978) was an outstanding left tackle. He was drafted as a defensive lineman but made a successful position change. He saw his career cut short after a blood clot in his brain required life-saving surgery. Elbert Drungo (1969–1977) starts at two positions on the All-Decade team—he was that good. Drungo was the Oilers' starting right tackle from 1973 to 1976 and was arguably Houston's most consistent lineman of the 1970s.

KICKER: Toni Fritsch (1977–1981) is the sixth most successful Oilers/Titans kicker in franchise history with 81 total field goals and ranks fourth among kickers with 100 or more field goal attempts with a 77.1% success rate.

KICK RETURNER: Billy "White Shoes" Johnson (1974–1980) returned two kickoffs for touchdowns in his first four seasons in Houston. He was selected to the Pro Bowl as a kick returner in 1975 and was named the MVP of the all-star game after returning a punt 90 yards for a score. Johnson is one of the greatest special teams players in NFL history.

Statistics for the all-decade team are for the given decade only, unless otherwise noted.

All-1970s Defense

DEFENSIVE ENDS: One of the greatest players in Oilers history, Elvin Bethea (1968–1983) made eight visits to the Pro Bowl. The NFL didn't officially begin tracking sacks until 1982. Nonetheless, he unofficially recorded 105 sacks, making him the franchise's all-time leader. Bethea was inducted into the Pro Football Hall of Fame in 2003. Tody Smith (1973–1976) accumulated 21 sacks in four seasons, including 10.5 sacks in 1974.

NOSE TACKLE: Houston's deal to acquire Curley Culp (1974–1980) from the Kansas City Chiefs was one of the greatest trades in Oilers history. Culp qualified for four consecutive Pro Bowls and was among the best defenders in the league. He was inducted into the Pro Football Hall of Fame in 2013.

LINEBACKERS: Robert Brazile (1975–1984) enjoyed instant success in the NFL, winning Defensive Rookie of the Year in 1975. He was one of the game's first great pass-rushing outside linebackers in a 3-4 defense and was inducted into the Pro Football Hall of Fame in 2018. Ted Washington (1973–1982) was one of the most underrated Oilers of all time. He compiled 45 sacks throughout his tenure with the team. Gregg Bingham (1973–1984) spent his entire 12-year career in Houston. He recorded 21 interceptions, 14.5 sacks, and 14 fumble recoveries. Steve Kiner (1974–1978) enjoyed five successful seasons during the best years of Bum Phillips' 3-4 defense.

CORNERBACKS: Zeke Moore (1967–1977) intercepted 24 career passes, was an AFL All-Star in 1969, and qualified for the Pro Bowl in 1970. Willie Alexander (1971–1979) was a starting cornerback during eight seasons. He intercepted 23 career passes.

SAFETIES: Ken Houston (1967–1972) is one of the NFL's all-time great safeties. He played just three seasons for the Oilers in the 1970s, but his impact was immeasurable. Houston was inducted into the Pro Football Hall of Fame in 1986. Mike Reinfeldt (1976–1983) was an elite ballhawk for Phillips' defense. His 12 interceptions in 1979 tied for most in a single season in franchise history.

PUNTER: Dan Pastorini (1971–1979) was the team's quarterback and punter for the majority of the decade. He ranks sixth in franchise history with 12,530 punt yards and fifth in total punts with 316.

PUNT RETURNER: Billy "White Shoes" Johnson (1974–1980) returned five punts for touchdowns in his first four seasons in Houston. He led the league in average per return twice and finished his time in Houston with an amazing 13.2 yards per return. Johnson is one of the greatest special teams players in NFL history.

Dan Pastorini started 107 games at quarterback in nine seasons with Houston.

1980

11–5

Second in AFC Central

In an attempt to leapfrog the Pittsburgh Steelers in the AFC Central, the Oilers made several personnel-related moves for the 1980 season. None was more notable than the acquisition of veteran quarterback Ken Stabler. In a rare quarterback-for-quarterback trade, the Oilers acquired Stabler from the Oakland Raiders in exchange for Dan Pastorini. A four-time Pro Bowl player, Super Bowl XI champion, and 1974 Most Valuable Player, Stabler seemed to be a more capable quarterback.

Unfortunately, he threw just 13 touchdowns, his lowest total since 1972. Meanwhile, Stabler's 28 interceptions were the second-highest total of his career. The veteran slinger struggled to acclimate to his new surroundings, and the Oilers scored a 20th-ranked 18.4 points per game. In an attempt to rejuvenate Stabler, the Oilers completed a second trade with the Raiders six games into the campaign, this time acquiring five-time Pro Bowl tight end Dave Casper in exchange for their 1981 first- and second-round draft picks.

Houston's offense was again spearheaded by running back Earl Campbell. Fresh off an MVP-winning season, Campbell continued to outdo himself. He rushed for a career-high 1,934 yards while averaging a personal-best 5.2 yards per attempt. Campbell won his third consecutive rushing title and a third straight award for NFL Offensive Player of the Year. He rushed for 200-plus yards four times, setting the NFL mark for most times in a season.

Age and injuries began taking a toll on veteran nose tackle Curley Culp. He recorded zero sacks in 10 regular-season appearances and was released from his contract. Culp finished the season with the Detroit Lions.

The Oilers won 11 games, but the Cleveland Browns took the division via tiebreaker, forcing the Oilers to settle for a wild-card spot. Coincidentally, they met the Raiders. A one-yard touchdown run by Campbell gave Houston an early 7–3 lead, but Oakland quarterback Jim Plunkett, who had replaced Pastorini as the starter due to injury, led his team to 24 unanswered points and a dominant victory, 27–7. The Raiders went on to win the Super Bowl—meaning the Oilers had been eliminated from the postseason by the eventual Super Bowl winners on three straight occasions.

Schedule

	OPPONENT	SCORE	RECORD
L	@ Pittsburgh Steelers	17–31	0–1
W	@ Cleveland Browns	16–7	1–1
W	Baltimore Colts	21–16	2–1
W	@ Cincinnati Bengals	13–10	3–1
L	Seattle Seahawks	7–26	3–2
L	@ Kansas City Chiefs	20–21	3–3
W	Tampa Bay Buccaneers	20–14	4–3
W	Cincinnati Bengals	23–3	5–3
W	@ Denver Broncos	20–16	6–3
W	New England Patriots	38–34	7–3
W	@ Chicago Bears	10–6	8–3
L	@ New York Jets (OT)	28–31	8–4
L	Cleveland Browns	14–17	8–5
W	Pittsburgh Steelers	6–0	9–5
W	@ Green Bay Packers	22–3	10–5
W	Minnesota Vikings	20–16	11–5
L	*@ Oakland Raiders*	*7–27*	*0–1*

Season Leaders

CATEGORY	TOTAL	PLAYER
Passing Yards	3,202	Ken Stabler
Rushing Yards	1,934	Earl Campbell
Receiving Yards	712	Mike Barber
Receptions	59	Mike Barber
Interceptions	7	Jack Tatum
Sacks	7	Mike Stensrud
Points	83	Toni Fritsch

Key Additions:
Ken Stabler (QB), Tim Smith (WR)

Starting Lineup

CB Greg Stemrick

Dave Casper TE

Leon Gray LT

LB Robert Brazile

Earl Campbell RB

DE Elvin Bethea

Bob Young LG

LB Daryl Hunt

SS Vernon Perry

Ken Stabler QB

Carl Mauck C

NT Ken Kennard

LB Gregg Bingham

FS Mike Reinfeldt

Ed Fisher RG

Tim Wilson RB

DE Andy Dorris

Morris Towns RT

LB Ted Washington

K Toni Fritsch
KR Carl Roaches
P Cliff Parsley
PR Carl Roaches

Mike Barber TE

Mike Renfro WR

CB J.C. Wilson

Titans Trivia

Over 80,000 fans watched the Oilers defeat the Browns at Cleveland Stadium—the largest crowd ever at an Oilers football game.

Pro Bowl Selections

- Robert Brazile (LB)
- Earl Campbell (RB)
- Dave Casper (TE)
- Greg Stemrick (CB)

1981

7–9
Third in AFC Central

Owner Bud Adams surprisingly fired general manager and head coach Bum Phillips after the 1980 season—just three days after the team's playoff loss to the Oakland Raiders. It was a controversial decision because Phillips had helped deliver Houston's best results since the early 1960s. The coach's dismissal stemmed from his refusal to hire an offensive coordinator.

Phillips did not remain unemployed for long. He was named the head coach of the New Orleans Saints just a few weeks later. In Week 12, his Saints defeated the Oilers, 27–24.

Executive vice president Ladd Herzeg was promoted to general manager, and Mike Holovak was named assistant general manager. Defensive coordinator Ed Biles was promoted to head coach. Dick Nolan, who had served as the head coach of the New Orleans Saints, was hired as the new defensive coordinator. Former Cleveland Browns quarterbacks coach Jim Shofner was named Houston's offensive coordinator.

Despite the shake-up—or perhaps because of it—the Oilers regressed in 1981. The offense did not improve. In fact, the team's points per game dropped from 18.4 to 17.6. Ken Stabler retired ahead of the season but returned to the team, which desperately needed a quarterback. Separate three-game losing streaks doomed the season. Biles' Oilers won just three of their final 10 contests, crawling to a disappointing record of 7–9. The Oilers missed the playoffs for the first time since 1977.

Earl Campbell rushed for an AFC-high 1,376 yards and added 10 rushing touchdowns to his offensive totals. Both marked career lows for Campbell.

The season ended on a high note, with the Oilers defeating the Pittsburgh Steelers, 21–20. Gifford Nielsen, who became Houston's starting quarterback at the end of the season, threw for 377 yards and three scores in the win.

Schedule

	OPPONENT	SCORE	RECORD
W	@ Los Angeles Rams	27–20	1–0
W	@ Cleveland Browns	9–3	2–0
L	Miami Dolphins	10–16	2–1
L	@ New York Jets	17–33	2–2
W	Cincinnati Bengals	17–10	3–2
W	Seattle Seahawks	35–17	4–2
L	@ New England Patriots	10–38	4–3
L	@ Pittsburgh Steelers	13–26	4–4
L	@ Cincinnati Bengals	21–34	4–5
W	Oakland Raiders	17–16	5–5
L	@ Kansas City Chiefs	10–23	5–6
L	New Orleans Saints	24–27	5–7
L	Atlanta Falcons	27–31	5–8
W	Cleveland Browns	17–13	6–8
L	@ San Francisco 49ers	6–28	6–9
W	Pittsburgh Steelers	21–20	7–9

Season Leaders

CATEGORY	TOTAL	PLAYER
Passing Yards	1,988	Ken Stabler
Rushing Yards	1,376	Earl Campbell
Receiving Yards	668	Ken Burrough
Receptions	40	Ken Burrough
Interceptions	3	C. Hartwig, G. Stemrick
Sacks	10	Jesse Baker
Points	77	Toni Fritsch

Pro Bowl Selections

- Robert Brazile (LB)
- Earl Campbell (RB)
- Leon Gray (OT)
- Carl Roaches (KR)

Key Additions:
Willie Tullis (CB/KR)

Starting Lineup

OFFENSE	POSITION
Ken Stabler	QB
Earl Campbell	RB
Tim Wilson	RB
Mike Renfro	WR
Ken Burrough	WR
Dave Casper	TE
Leon Gray	LT
John Schuhmacher	LG
David Carter	C
Ed Fisher	RG
Morris Towns	RT

DEFENSE	POSITION
Andy Dorris	DE
Ken Kennard	NT
Elvin Bethea	DE
Ted Washington	OLB
Gregg Bingham	ILB
Daryl Hunt	ILB
Robert Brazile	OLB
J.C. Wilson	CB
Greg Stemrick	CB
Vernon Perry	SS
Mike Reinfeldt	FS

SPECIAL TEAMS	POSITION
Toni Fritsch	K
Willie Tullis	KR
Cliff Parsley	P
Carl Roaches	PR

Gregg Bingham (54) missed just two starts for Houston throughout his 12-year career.

1982

1–8
Fourth in AFC Central

The 1982 season was marked by change. Retired legendary safety Ken Houston rejoined the Oilers on head coach Ed Biles' defensive staff. Dick Nolan did not return as the defensive coordinator, nor did Biles name a replacement. Ken Stabler, who had been the starting quarterback in 1980 and 1981, was released from his contract, and wide receiver Ken Burrough retired. His 408 receptions rank seventh all-time in Oilers/Titans history. He's also third in receiving yards with 6,906, and his 47 receiving touchdowns are tied for second most. Burrough was one of the greatest players in franchise history.

Houston's biggest win of the year came before the season started: in the 1982 NFL Draft. With the eighth overall selection, the Oilers picked guard Mike Munchak. He would quickly develop into an elite player.

Coming off a stellar end to the 1981 season, Gifford Nielsen was named the starting quarterback. But following a blowout defeat to the Cincinnati Bengals in Week 1, the Oilers acquired quarterback Archie Manning from the Saints in exchange for Pro Bowl left tackle Leon Gray.

NFL players agreed to embark on a league-wide strike just two games into the 1982 campaign. Various disagreements, including one over revenue sharing, led to the dispute. The stoppage lasted from September 20 to November 16 and shortened the season to nine games.

Manning replaced Nielsen as the starting quarterback after three games. Manning went on to start five consecutive games—and went 0–5—before Nielsen finished the season against the Bengals.

The 1982 Oilers were miserable. Their 24th-ranked offense scored 15.1 points per game. Their leaky defense allowed a second-worst 27.2 points per contest. The forgettable team finished 1–8, their first one-win season since 1973.

Pro Bowl Selections

- Robert Brazile (LB)

Schedule

	OPPONENT	SCORE	RECORD
L	@ Cincinnati Bengals	6–27	0–1
W	Seattle Seahawks	23–21	1–1
L	Pittsburgh Steelers	10–24	1–2
L	@ New England Patriots	21–29	1–3
L	@ New York Giants	14–17	1–4
L	Dallas Cowboys	7–37	1–5
L	@ Philadelphia Eagles	14–35	1–6
L	Cleveland Browns	14–20	1–7
L	Cincinnati Bengals	27–35	1–8

Season Leaders

CATEGORY	TOTAL	PLAYER
Passing Yards	1,005	Gifford Nielsen
Rushing Yards	538	Earl Campbell
Receiving Yards	573	Dave Casper
Receptions	36	Dave Casper
Interceptions	1	Three players tied
Sacks	7.5	Jesse Baker
Points	36	Dave Casper

Key Additions:
Mike Munchak (G)

Starting Lineup

OFFENSE	POSITION
Archie Manning	QB
Earl Campbell	RB
Stan Edwards	RB
Mike Renfro	WR
Harold Bailey	WR
Dave Casper	TE
John Schuhmacher	LT
Ralph Williams	LG
David Carter	C
Ed Fisher	RG
Morris Towns	RT

DEFENSE	POSITION
Ken Kennard	DE
Mike Stensrud	NT
Jesse Baker	DE
Avon Riley	OLB
Gregg Bingham	ILB
Daryl Hunt	ILB
Robert Brazile	OLB
J.C. Wilson	CB
Greg Stemrick	CB
Vernon Perry	SS
Mike Reinfeldt	FS

SPECIAL TEAMS	POSITION
Florian Kempf	K
Carl Roaches	KR
John James	P
Carl Roaches	PR

"Somebody will always break your records. It is how you live that counts."

—Earl Campbell

Robert Brazile was named to seven straight Pro Bowls (1976–1982).

1983

2–14
Fourth in AFC Central

Several notable veterans departed the Oilers following the 1982 season. After spending his entire 10-year career in Houston, linebacker Ted Washington retired. Cornerback Greg Stemrick reunited with Bum Phillips by joining the New Orleans Saints, as did safety Vernon Perry.

Former San Francisco 49ers defensive coordinator Chuck Studley was named the Oilers' new defensive coordinator by head coach Ed Biles. Veteran coach Kay Dalton was named offensive coordinator.

For the second straight year, Oilers general manager Ladd Herzeg selected an interior offensive lineman with a top-10 draft pick. Guard Bruce Matthews was the ninth overall selection in the 1983 NFL Draft. The Oilers originally owned the second selection, but they traded down twice and added multiple mid-round picks in 1983 and 1984. Along with the addition of Matthews, rookie Harvey Salem became the starting right tackle. Safety Keith Bostic, cornerback Steve Brown, and tight end Chris Dressel were also immediate contributors in their rookie seasons.

After an 0–6 start, Biles resigned. In two-and-a-half seasons, he compiled a lackluster record of 8–23. His .258 win percentage ranks among the worst in franchise history. Studley was named his interim replacement.

The Oilers began selling off assets for future draft capital. Following a Week 7 defeat to the Minnesota Vikings, the Oilers traded quarterback Archie Manning and veteran tight end Dave Casper to the Vikings in exchange for second- and fourth-round picks in the 1984 NFL Draft.

The Oilers finished 2–14, but the young team offered glimmers of hope. Matthews and Salem qualified for the NFL All-Rookie team.

Defensive end Elvin Bethea retired at the conclusion of the 1983 season. Bethea qualified for eight Pro Bowls throughout his illustrious 16-year career with the Oilers. He played in 210 games for Houston, and his 105 sacks rank as the most in franchise history. Bethea's number 65 jersey was retired by the club, and he was inducted into the Pro Football Hall of Fame in 2003.

Schedule

	OPPONENT	SCORE	RECORD
L	Green Bay Packers (OT)	38–41	0–1
L	@ Los Angeles Raiders	6–20	0–2
L	Pittsburgh Steelers	28–40	0–3
L	@ Buffalo Bills	13–30	0–4
L	@ Pittsburgh Steelers	10–17	0–5
L	Denver Broncos	14–26	0–6
L	@ Minnesota Vikings	14–34	0–7
L	Kansas City Chiefs (OT)	10–13	0–8
L	@ Cleveland Browns (OT)	19–25	0–9
L	Cincinnati Bengals	14–55	0–10
W	Detroit Lions	27–17	1–10
L	@ Cincinnati Bengals	10–38	1–11
L	@ Tampa Bay Buccaneers	24–33	1–12
L	Miami Dolphins	17–24	1–13
W	Cleveland Browns	34–27	2–13
L	@ Baltimore Colts	10–20	2–14

Season Leaders

CATEGORY	TOTAL	PLAYER
Passing Yards	1,375	Oliver Luck
Rushing Yards	1,301	Earl Campbell
Receiving Yards	1,176	Tim Smith
Receptions	83	Tim Smith
Interceptions	5	Willie Tullis
Sacks	5.5	Jesse Baker
Points	84	Florian Kempf

Key Additions:
Keith Bostic (S), Steve Brown (CB), Bruce Matthews (G)

Starting Lineup

Titans Trivia

From 1978 to 1983, the Oilers made just three first-round picks: Earl Campbell (1978), Mike Munchak (1982), and Bruce Matthews (1983).

Pro Bowl Selections

- Earl Campbell (RB)

66
74

M & M

The Houston Oilers selected future hall-of-fame offensive linemen in consecutive drafts. Mike Munchak was chosen with the eighth overall pick in 1982, and Bruce Matthews was taken with the ninth pick in 1983. Together, they developed into two of the best offensive linemen in NFL history, while giving the Oilers a hard-nosed identity.

The franchise hit its stride in the late 1980s with Matthews and Munchak serving as hallmark players. The Oilers made seven consecutive playoff appearances between 1987 and 1993, winning three postseason games in the process. Munchak was an All-Pro selection every year during that span, and Matthews most likely would have matched that honor if not for a contract dispute in 1987. Matthews began a streak of 14 consecutive Pro Bowls a year later, in 1988.

Munchak played his entire 12-year career with the Oilers, becoming the first hall-of-fame player to spend his entire career with Houston. His number 63 jersey hangs in the rafters, and he is a member of the Pro Football Hall of Fame.

While Munchak retired following the 1993 campaign, Matthews continued playing at a high level through 2001, helping his team advance to the Super Bowl in 1999. Matthews appeared in 296 career games, including a franchise-record 229 consecutive starts. He became the first "Tennessee Titans" player to gain entrance into the Pro Football Hall of Fame. His number 74 jersey was retired by the club.

Munchak is a member of the NFL All-Decade Team for the 1980s. Matthews received the same honor for the NFL All-Decade Team of the 1990s. Along with legendary running back Earl Campbell, they are arguably the greatest players in franchise history.

Bruce Matthews (74) and Mike Munchak (63) combined to make 327 appearances between 1982 and 1993.

1984

3–13

Fourth in AFC Central

With the second overall pick in the 1984 NFL Draft, general manager Ladd Herzeg chose offensive tackle Dean Steinkuhler. It represented the third consecutive draft in which the Oilers selected an offensive lineman in the top 10, following the selections of Mike Munchak (1982) and Bruce Matthews (1983). Steinkuhler would be a regular starter through the rest of the decade.

Interim head coach Chuck Studley was replaced by Hugh Campbell for the 1984 season. Campbell had previously spent time with Edmonton of the Canadian Football League (CFL). Campbell retained Kay Dalton as his offensive coordinator, and he hired Jerry Glanville to be his defensive coordinator.

Campbell's appointment as the head coach had clear intentions behind it. His prolific CFL quarterback, Warren Moon, decided to make the jump to the NFL. Moon had led Edmonton to five consecutive Grey Cups (Canada's version of the Super Bowl) between 1978 and 1982. Campbell's presence helped the Oilers lure Moon—who had several NFL suitors—to Houston.

Moon and the Oilers struggled throughout their first campaign together. They began the season with a 10-game losing streak for the second year in a row. Realizing the roster rebuild was far from complete, after six games, the Oilers traded superstar running back Earl Campbell to the New Orleans Saints in exchange for a first-round pick in the 1985 NFL Draft. Campbell was averaging a career-low 2.9 yards per carry.

Campbell is among the greatest players in franchise history. When he retired following the 1985 season, he was the league's seventh all-time leading rusher. He was inducted into the Pro Football Hall of Fame in 1991 and the Oilers/Titans Hall of Fame in 1999.

The Oilers finished the 1984 season 3–13. Moon threw more interceptions (14) than touchdowns (12). While the season was a disappointment, various young players were now in place to achieve future success.

Munchak qualified for his first Pro Bowl and officially took his place as one of the best guards in the league.

Schedule

	OPPONENT	SCORE	RECORD
L	Los Angeles Raiders	14–24	0–1
L	Indianapolis Colts	21–35	0–2
L	@ San Diego Chargers	14–31	0–3
L	@ Atlanta Falcons	10–42	0–4
L	New Orleans Saints	10–27	0–5
L	@ Cincinnati Bengals	3–13	0–6
L	@ Miami Dolphins	10–28	0–7
L	San Francisco 49ers	21–34	0–8
L	Cincinnati Bengals	13–31	0–9
L	@ Pittsburgh Steelers	7–35	0–10
W	@ Kansas City Chiefs	17–16	1–10
W	New York Jets	31–20	2–10
L	@ Cleveland Browns	10–27	2–11
W	Pittsburgh Steelers (OT)	23–20	3–11
L	@ Los Angeles Rams	16–27	3–12
L	Cleveland Browns	20–27	3–13

Season Leaders

CATEGORY	TOTAL	PLAYER
Passing Yards	3,338	Warren Moon
Rushing Yards	785	Larry Moriarty
Receiving Yards	1,141	Tim Smith
Receptions	69	Tim Smith
Interceptions	4	Willie Tullis
Sacks	11	Jesse Baker
Points	46	Joe Cooper

Key Additions:
Patrick Allen (CB), Jeff Donaldson (S), Johnny Meads (LB), Warren Moon (QB), Dean Steinkuhler (T)

Starting Lineup

Titans Trivia

Warren Moon was inducted into the Canadian Football Hall of Fame in 2001.

Pro Bowl Selections

- Mike Munchak (G)

1985

5–11
Fourth in AFC Central

A pair of highly respected defensive veterans departed from the Oilers before the 1985 campaign. Robert "Dr. Doom" Brazile retired at the conclusion of the 1984 season, following his wife's tragic passing. A focal point of Bum Phillips' 3-4 defensive scheme, Brazile was inducted into the Pro Football Hall of Fame and Oilers/Titans Ring of Honor in 2018. Linebacker Gregg Bingham also retired after the 1984 season. Bingham appeared in 173 career games for the Oilers. He totaled 21 interceptions and recovered 14 fumbles.

General manager Ladd Herzeg began revamping the defense by selecting defensive end Ray Childress with the third overall pick in the 1985 NFL Draft. Then, with the first-round selection acquired from the New Orleans Saints in the Earl Campbell trade, the Oilers selected cornerback Richard Johnson. The Oilers also added Mike Rozier to their offense. A punishing fullback, Rozier had been chosen second overall in the NFL's supplemental draft of players from the United States Football League (USFL) and Canadian Football League (CFL) before the 1984 season. Rozier joined the team a year later. He rushed for a team-high 462 yards and eight touchdowns.

Veteran wide receiver Drew Hill was acquired from the Los Angeles Rams via trade. Hill, who never topped 500 yards in five seasons with Los Angeles, immediately showcased his chemistry with Warren Moon. He recorded his first 1,000-yard season, gaining 1,169 yards on 64 receptions.

Despite Hill's emergence, Houston's offense underperformed. New offensive coordinator Joe Faragalli had previously worked with Moon and head coach Hugh Campbell in the CFL. Yet the Oilers scored 13 or fewer points in three of their first four games.

A midseason three-game winning streak hinted at the team's potential. Hill showed off his consistency, catching 17 passes for 278 yards and scoring a touchdown in each of those games.

The Oilers' record fell to 5–9, following a blowout loss to the New York Giants, 35–14, in early December. With two games to go, Hugh Campbell was relieved of his duties. He was replaced by defensive coordinator Jerry Glanville on an interim basis.

Schedule

	OPPONENT	SCORE	RECORD
W	Miami Dolphins	26–23	1–0
L	@ Washington	13–16	1–1
L	@ Pittsburgh Steelers	0–20	1–2
L	Dallas Cowboys	10–17	1–3
L	@ Denver Broncos	20–31	1–4
L	Cleveland Browns	6–21	1–5
W	Cincinnati Bengals	44–27	2–5
W	@ Saint Louis Cardinals	20–10	3–5
W	Kansas City Chiefs	23–20	4–5
L	@ Buffalo Bills	0–20	4–6
L	Pittsburgh Steelers	7–30	4–7
W	San Diego Chargers	37–35	5–7
L	@ Cincinnati Bengals	27–45	5–8
L	New York Giants	14–35	5–9
L	@ Cleveland Browns	21–28	5–10
L	@ Indianapolis Colts	16–34	5–11

Season Leaders

CATEGORY	TOTAL	PLAYER
Passing Yards	2,709	Warren Moon
Rushing Yards	462	Mike Rozier
Receiving Yards	1,169	Drew Hill
Receptions	80	Butch Woolfolk
Interceptions	5	Steve Brown
Sacks	5.5	Jesse Baker
Points	92	Tony Zendejas

Key Additions:
Ray Childress (DE), Drew Hill (WR), Mike Rozier (RB)

Starting Lineup

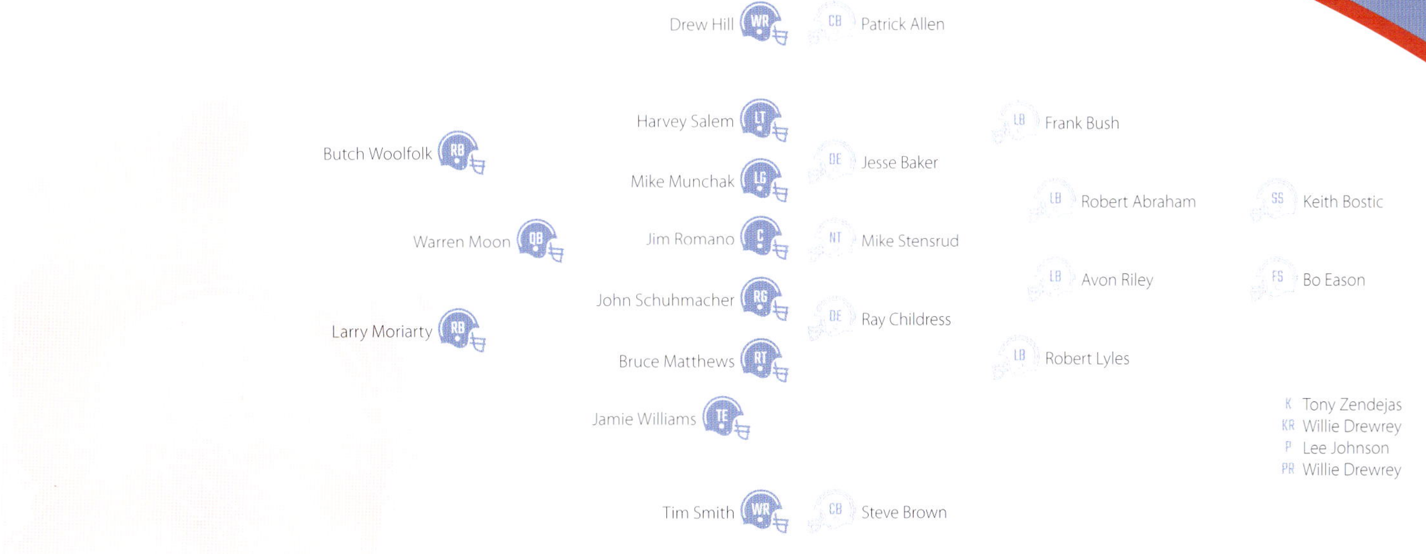

Titans Trivia

Through his short-lived tenure, Hugh Campbell's Oilers were outscored 787–487.

Pro Bowl Selections

- Mike Munchak (G)

1986

5-11
Fourth in AFC Central

Despite losing his two games as interim head coach in 1985, former defensive coordinator Jerry Glanville was named the team's head coach ahead of 1986. Glanville signed a five-year contract and began revamping his coaching staff by naming Dick Jamieson as offensive coordinator. Floyd Reese was hired as linebackers coach. (Reese would later become a prominent figure in the franchise's history as the team's general manager.) Steve Watterson was hired as strength and conditioning coach, a post he'd legendarily hold until the conclusion of the 2017 season.

The Oilers picked quarterback Jim Everett with the third overall selection in the 1986 NFL Draft. With franchise quarterback Warren Moon already in place, it was seen by most as a peculiar pick. However, it worked out well. When Everett and the Oilers failed to reach a contract agreement, the Oilers flipped Everett to the Los Angeles Rams in exchange for Pro Bowl guard Kent Hill, defensive end William Fuller, first-round picks in 1987 and 1988, and a fifth-round selection in 1987.

In the second round, Houston picked wide receiver Ernest Givins, who immediately developed into an elite contributor.

The Oilers began the 1986 campaign in impressive fashion, defeating the Green Bay Packers, 31–3, on opening weekend. This immediate success didn't last. Glanville's Oilers lost eight consecutive games and crawled to a record of 5–11 for a second straight season.

Moon finished the year with 3,489 passing yards, the seventh-highest single-season total of his career. Wide receivers Drew Hill and Ernest Givins became just the second Oilers duo to each account for 1,000 receiving yards. Hill led the team with 1,112, and Givins kept pace with 1,062.

The puzzle pieces were in place to field a more successful offense.

Pro Bowl Selections

- None

Schedule

	OPPONENT	SCORE	RECORD
W	@ Green Bay Packers	31–3	1–0
L	Cleveland Browns	20–23	1–1
L	@ Kansas City Chiefs	13–27	1–2
L	Pittsburgh Steelers (OT)	16–22	1–3
L	@ Detroit Lions	13–24	1–4
L	Chicago Bears	7–20	1–5
L	@ Cincinnati Bengals	28–31	1–6
L	Los Angeles Raiders	17–28	1–7
L	@ Miami Dolphins	7–28	1–8
W	Cincinnati Bengals	32–28	2–8
L	@ Pittsburgh Steelers	10–21	2–9
W	Indianapolis Colts	31–17	3–9
L	@ Cleveland Browns (OT)	10–13	3–10
L	@ San Diego Chargers	0–27	3–11
W	Minnesota Vikings	23–10	4–11
W	Buffalo Bills	16–7	5–11

Season Leaders

CATEGORY	TOTAL	PLAYER
Passing Yards	3,489	Warren Moon
Rushing Yards	662	Mike Rozier
Receiving Yards	1,112	Drew Hill
Receptions	65	Drew Hill
Interceptions	3	Patrick Allen, Allen Lyday
Sacks	5	Ray Childress
Points	94	Tony Zendejas

Key Additions:
William Fuller (DE), Ernest Givins (WR), Jay Pennison (C)

Ernest Givins is the franchise's all-time leader in receiving yards (7,935).

Starting Lineup

OFFENSE	POSITION
Warren Moon	QB
Mike Rozier	RB
Larry Moriarty	RB
Drew Hill	WR
Ernest Givins	WR
Jamie Williams	TE
Bruce Matthews	LT
Mike Munchak	LG
Jim Romano	C
Kent Hill	RG
Dean Steinkuhler	RT

DEFENSE	POSITION
Ray Childress	DE
Mike Golic	NT
Richard Byrd	DE
Robert Lyles	OLB
John Grimsley	ILB
Robert Abraham	ILB
Johnny Meads	OLB
Steve Brown	CB
Patrick Allen	CB
Keith Bostic	SS
Bo Eason	FS

SPECIAL TEAMS	POSITION
Tony Zendejas	K
Allen Pinkett	KR
Lee Johnson	P
Willie Drewrey	PR

1987

9–6

Second in AFC Central

The Oilers drafted fullback Alonzo Highsmith with the third overall selection in the 1987 NFL Draft. However, a lengthy contract-related holdout kept Highsmith sidelined for the first seven games of the season. With the 20th overall selection, a pick the Oilers acquired from the Los Angeles Rams in the Jim Everett deal, general manager Ladd Herzeg selected wide receiver Haywood Jeffires.

The Oilers began the season 1–1, but a league-wide players strike canceled all Week 3 contests; the season was shortened from 16 games to 15. The labor conflict progressed to a strike, and the league opted to use replacement players. The strike lasted 24 days, and replacement players filled in for three games, during which the Oilers went 2–1.

An additional contract-related dispute took place with offensive lineman Bruce Matthews. He held out for the first half of the season but finally signed an extension with the Oilers in November, one day after the team acquired offensive tackle Bruce Davis from the Los Angeles Raiders.

Despite the multitude of distractions that could have derailed the season, the team rumbled to a 9–6 finish, clinching their first postseason berth since 1980. In the wild-card round of the playoffs, the Oilers hosted the Seattle Seahawks. Moon threw a 29-yard touchdown pass to receiver Willie Drewrey, giving Houston a 20–13 lead in the fourth quarter. But Seattle tied the game to force overtime. Not to be denied, the Oilers won on a dramatic 42-yard field goal by Tony Zendejas—his third field goal from over 40 yards in the game.

Houston's run ended in the divisional round with a 34–10 blowout loss to the Denver Broncos. Moon was intercepted twice, while Broncos quarterback John Elway threw for 259 yards and two touchdowns.

Houston's offense fielded a top-10 scoring unit, and quarterback Warren Moon threw for 21 touchdowns. Running back Mike Rozier rushed for 957 yards, while wide receivers Drew Hill and Ernest Givins both gained more than 900 yards receiving—all in just 12 games. The Oilers were a young team on the rise.

Schedule

	OPPONENT	SCORE	RECORD
W	Los Angeles Rams	20–16	1–0
L	@ Buffalo Bills	30–34	1–1
W	@ Denver Broncos	40–10	2–1
W	@ Cleveland Browns	15–10	3–1
L	New England Patriots	7–21	3–2
W	Atlanta Falcons	37–33	4–2
W	@ Cincinnati Bengals	31–29	5–2
L	@ San Francisco 49ers	20–27	5–3
W	@ Pittsburgh Steelers	23–3	6–3
L	Cleveland Browns	7–40	6–4
L	@ Indianapolis Colts	27–51	6–5
W	San Diego Chargers	33–18	7–5
L	@ New Orleans Saints	10–24	7–6
W	Pittsburgh Steelers	24–16	8–6
W	Cincinnati Bengals	21–17	9–6
W	*Seattle Seahawks (OT)*	*23–20*	*1–0*
L	*@ Denver Broncos*	*10–34*	*1–1*

Season Leaders

CATEGORY	TOTAL	PLAYER
Passing Yards	2,806	Warren Moon
Rushing Yards	957	Mike Rozier
Receiving Yards	989	Drew Hill
Receptions	53	Ernest Givins
Interceptions	6	Keith Bostic
Sacks	6	Ray Childress
Points	92	Tony Zendejas

Key Additions:
Bruce Davis (OT), Curtis Duncan (WR), Haywood Jeffires (WR), Al Smith (LB)

Starting Lineup

Titans Trivia

Brent Pease served as Houston's quarterback during the strike. In his first start, he threw for 260 yards and accounted for two touchdowns.

Pro Bowl Selections

- Keith Bostic (S)
- Mike Munchak (G)
- Mike Rozier (RB)

1988

10–6
Third in AFC Central

Staying aggressive in pursuit of improvement, general manager Ladd Herzeg traded one of his two first-round selections (ninth overall), along with third- and fourth-round picks, to the Los Angeles Raiders in exchange for veteran defensive end Sean Jones and second- and third-round picks. Jones was a proven sack artist who had recorded 15.5 quarterback takedowns in 1986. In the fifth round, Herzeg drafted cornerback Cris Dishman, who would develop into a steal for the franchise.

Several assistant coaches joined Jerry Glanville's staff, including defensive backs coach Nick Saban. He would spend two seasons with the Oilers and would eventually become one of the greatest college football coaches of all time at the University of Alabama.

An explosive offense carried the Oilers through 1988, despite quarterback Warren Moon suffering a shoulder injury in the regular-season opener that caused him to miss six games. The Oilers averaged a second-ranked 26.5 points per contest. Wide receiver Drew Hill recorded 72 receptions for 1,141 yards and 10 touchdowns, becoming the team's first receiver to catch 10 or more touchdowns in a season since 1966. Running back Mike Rozier rushed for 1,002 yards and 10 touchdowns, the franchise's best since 1983.

In the wild-card round of the playoffs, Houston faced their AFC Central rivals the Cleveland Browns. Oilers running back Allen Pinkett scored two second-quarter touchdowns. A late Cleveland touchdown wasn't enough, as Houston held on to win, 24–23.

Houston's season came to a hard-fought end a week later. The Oilers fumbled five times, losing two, and Moon threw an interception. Houston's offense was stifled by the Buffalo Bills, who won the game, 17–10

Pro Bowl Selections

- Keith Bostic (S)
- Ray Childress (DE)
- John Grimsley (LB)
- Drew Hill (WR)
- Bruce Matthews (G)
- Warren Moon (QB)
- Mike Munchak (G)
- Mike Rozier (RB)

Schedule

	OPPONENT	SCORE	RECORD
W	@ Indianapolis Colts (OT)	17–14	1–0
W	Los Angeles Raiders	38–35	2–0
L	@ New York Jets	3–45	2–1
W	New England Patriots	31–6	3–1
L	@ Philadelphia Eagles	23–32	3–2
W	Kansas City Chiefs	7–6	4–2
W	@ Pittsburgh Steelers	34–14	5–2
L	@ Cincinnati Bengals	21–44	5–3
W	Washington	41–17	6–3
W	Cleveland Browns	24–17	7–3
L	@ Seattle Seahawks	24–27	7–4
W	Phoenix Cardinals	38–20	8–4
W	@ Dallas Cowboys	25–17	9–4
L	Pittsburgh Steelers	34–37	9–5
W	Cincinnati Bengals	41–6	10–5
L	@ Cleveland Browns	23–28	10–6
W	*@ Cleveland Browns*	*24–23*	*1–0*
L	*@ Buffalo Bills*	*10–17*	*1–1*

Season Leaders

CATEGORY	TOTAL	PLAYER
Passing Yards	2,327	Warren Moon
Rushing Yards	1,002	Mike Rozier
Receiving Yards	1,141	Drew Hill
Receptions	72	Drew Hill
Interceptions	4	Jeff Donaldson
Sacks	8.5	R. Childress, W. Fuller
Points	114	Tony Zendejas

Key Additions:
Cris Dishman (CB), Sean Jones (DE), Greg Montgomery (P), Lorenzo White (RB)

Starting Lineup

OFFENSE	POSITION
Warren Moon	QB
Mike Rozier	RB
Alonzo Highsmith	RB
Drew Hill	WR
Ernest Givins	WR
Jamie Williams	TE
Bruce Davis	LT
Mike Munchak	LG
Jay Pennison	C
Bruce Matthews	RG
Dean Steinkuhler	RT

DEFENSE	POSITION
Ray Childress	DE
Doug Smith	NT
William Fuller	DE
Robert Lyles	OLB
John Grimsley	ILB
Al Smith	ILB
Johnny Meads	OLB
Steve Brown	CB
Patrick Allen	CB
Keith Bostic	SS
Jeff Donaldson	FS

SPECIAL TEAMS	POSITION
Tony Zendejas	K
Leonard Harris	KR
Greg Montgomery	P
Kenny Johnson	PR

Ray Childress was named to his first of five career Pro Bowls in 1988.

1989

9–7

Second in AFC Central

The league announced Plan B free agency, which allowed each team to retain limited rights to 37 players each season. A team had the first chance to re-sign a player and would receive compensation from another team if the player signed elsewhere. Quarterback Warren Moon inked a multi-year contract extension, but notable departures included tight end Jamie Williams, safety Keith Bostic, and fullback Ray Wallace. Rookie safety Bubba McDowell and rookie tight end Bob Mrosko became immediate starters. The team's first-round pick, offensive tackle David Williams, began his career as a backup.

The league also installed developmental squads, better known today as practice squads. This permitted teams to sign five to seven additional first-year players.

Despite an abundance of upheaval, the Oilers' starting lineup was left largely unchanged from 1988. The offense fielded a top-10 scoring unit for a third consecutive campaign, averaging a seventh-ranked 22.8 points per game.

The 9–6 Oilers entered their regular-season finale versus the Cleveland Browns with the AFC Central Division title on the line. Moon completed 32 of 51 passes for 414 yards, two touchdowns, and one interception. Despite setting single-game career highs in multiple categories, Moon couldn't lead the Oilers to victory. The Browns prevailed, 24–20.

Houston had to settle for a wild-card spot again. They hosted their fellow AFC Central rival Pittsburgh Steelers. Thanks to two touchdown passes from Moon to wide receiver Ernest Givins, Houston battled to a 23–23 tie. The Oilers gave Pittsburgh good field position in overtime after Lorenzo White fumbled. Kicker Gary Anderson connected on a 50-yard attempt, and the Oilers' season was over—yet another difficult postseason exit.

Warren Moon threw for 3,631 yards in 1989, setting a new franchise single-season record. After three straight wild-card seasons, the Oilers hoped a new decade would lead to even greater success.

General manager Ladd Herzeg stepped down after the 1989 season. Assistant general manager Mike Holovak was promoted as Herzeg's replacement.

Schedule

	OPPONENT	SCORE	RECORD
L	@ Minnesota Vikings	7–38	0–1
W	@ San Diego Chargers	34–27	1–1
L	Buffalo Bills (OT)	41–47	1–2
W	Miami Dolphins	39–7	2–2
L	@ New England Patriots	13–23	2–3
W	@ Chicago Bears	33–28	3–3
W	Pittsburgh Steelers	27–0	4–3
L	@ Cleveland Browns	17–28	4–4
W	Detroit Lions	35–31	5–4
W	Cincinnati Bengals	26–24	6–4
W	Los Angeles Raiders	23–7	7–4
L	@ Kansas City Chiefs	0–34	7–5
W	@ Pittsburgh Steelers	23–16	8–5
W	Tampa Bay Buccaneers	20–17	9–5
L	@ Cincinnati Bengals	7–61	9–6
L	Cleveland Browns	20–24	9–7
L	*Pittsburgh Steelers (OT)*	*23–26*	*0–1*

Season Leaders

CATEGORY	TOTAL	PLAYER
Passing Yards	3,631	Warren Moon
Rushing Yards	531	Alonzo Highsmith
Receiving Yards	938	Drew Hill
Receptions	66	Drew Hill
Interceptions	5	Steve Brown
Sacks	8.5	Ray Childress
Points	115	Tony Zendejas

Key Additions:
Bubba McDowell (S), Glenn Montgomery (DT), David Williams (OT)

Starting Lineup

Drew Hill WR
CB Patrick Allen

Bruce Davis LT
LB Johnny Meads
Mike Rozier RB
DE William Fuller
Mike Munchak LG
LB Al Smith
SS Bubba McDowell
Warren Moon QB
Jay Pennison C
NT Doug Smith
LB John Grimsley
FS Jeff Donaldson
Bruce Matthews RG
DE Ray Childress
Alonzo Highsmith RB
Dean Steinkuhler RT
LB Robert Lyles
Bob Mrosko TE

K Tony Zendejas
KR Kenny Johnson
P Greg Montgomery
PR Kenny Johnson

Ernest Givins WR
CB Steve Brown

Titans Trivia

Houston shattered its previous single-season attendance record in 1989. The average home crowd was 56,378 fans per game.

Pro Bowl Selections

- Bruce Matthews (G)
- Warren Moon (QB)
- Mike Munchak (G)

All-1980s Offense

QUARTERBACK: Warren Moon (1984–1993) ranks first all-time in Oilers/Titans history in several statistical categories, including passing yards (33,685) and passing touchdowns (196). Moon led the Oilers to three straight playoff appearances to end the decade. He was inducted into the Pro Football of Fame in 2006 and is a member of the Oilers/Titans Ring of Honor.

RUNNING BACKS: Earl Campbell (1978–1984) produced the three best rushing campaigns of the decade. It began with a career-high 1,934 yards in 1980. He also rushed for 1,376 yards in 1981 and 1,301 yards in 1983. He is arguably the greatest Oiler of all time. Mike Rozier (1985–1990) rushed for 3,384 yards in the 1980s and added 595 receiving yards. He was named to two Pro Bowls.

WIDE RECEIVERS: The 1980s saw the best wide receiver duo in franchise history. Ernest Givins (1986–1994) was only the second Oilers receiver ever to gain 1,000 yards as a rookie. He never reached 1,000 yards again, but he remained a consistent weapon. He ranks first in franchise history in receptions (542) and receiving yards (7,935). Drew Hill (1985–1991) recorded three of his five 1,000-yard seasons during the 1980s. He ranks second all-time in franchise receiving yards (7,477), tied for second in receiving touchdowns (47), and fourth in receptions (480).

TIGHT END: Dave Casper and Mike Barber garnered consideration, but Jamie Williams (1984–1988) arguably meant more to his team's success. He had more than 1,400 receiving yards and scored eight touchdowns. He often did the "little things" that helped Warren Moon and the offense click in the mid-1980s.

CENTER: A true underdog that previously enjoyed a stint in the United States Football League (USFL), Jay Pennison (1986–1990) played on some outstanding offensive lines. The Oilers qualified for the postseason in four of Pennison's five seasons with the team.

GUARDS: Mike Munchak (1982–1993) qualified for five Pro Bowls from 1984 to 1989. He was a second-team selection for the NFL's 1980s All-Decade Team. Bruce Matthews (1983–2001) is among the greatest offensive linemen ever to play. A do-it-all blocker, Matthews moved around the Oilers' offensive line as needed, starting games at all five positions throughout his illustrious career. Matthews qualified for 14 Pro Bowls consecutively from 1988 to 2001.

TACKLES: Dean Steinkuhler (1984–1991) was the second overall draft pick in 1984. He never quite achieved his pre-draft expectations, but he made the All-Rookie Team and started 69 games during the 1980s. The Oilers doubled down on offensive linemen by selecting Harvey Salem (1983–1986) one round after picking Bruce Matthews in 1983. Salem was selected to the All-Rookie Team that year.

KICKER: In 1986, Tony Zendejas (1985–1990) set a club record for the most field goals made in a season with 22. He ranks fifth on the Oilers/Titans all-time scoring leader board with 548 points.

KICK RETURNER: Carl Roaches (1980–1984) was a kick returner in Houston for five seasons. He qualified for the Pro Bowl in 1981. He ranks third all-time in franchise history in kick return yards (3,276).

Statistics for the all-decade team are for the given decade only, unless otherwise noted.

All-1980s Defense

DEFENSIVE ENDS: Jesse Baker (1979–1987) led the Oilers in sacks for five consecutive seasons, from 1981 to 1985. He had 10 sacks in 1981 and 11 sacks in 1984. The third overall draft pick in 1985, Ray Childress (1985–1995) dominated the latter half of the decade, leading the Oilers defense in quarterback takedowns for four straight campaigns, from 1986 to 1989. He was selected to the Pro Bowl in 1988.

NOSE TACKLE: Mike Stensrud (1979–1985) edges out Doug Smith as Houston's top nose tackle of the decade. Stensrud led the Oilers in sacks during the 1980 season with seven. Stensrud was a mainstay through the first half of the decade, accumulating 24 sacks in six seasons.

LINEBACKERS: Robert Brazile (1975–1984) had his best seasons in the 1970s, but he recorded 6.5 sacks in 1980 and in 1982, and he qualified for Pro Bowls in 1980, 1981, and 1982. He played his entire career for the Oilers, unofficially finishing with 48 sacks. Johnny Meads (1984–1992) was a steady performer from 1984 through the conclusion of the decade. He enjoyed his most successful stretch from 1987 to 1989, recording 16 sacks in that span, including a career-high eight sacks in 1988. John Grimsley (1984–1990) and Al Smith (1987–1996) were Houston's primary starters at inside linebacker during the team's playoff appearances in the late 1980s. Grimsley made a Pro Bowl appearance in 1988. Smith amassed nearly 200 tackles across his first two seasons. He would go on to gain league-wide notoriety for his stellar play.

CORNERBACKS: Steve Brown (1983–1990) and Patrick Allen (1984–1990) were in lockstep for nearly their entire careers. Brown entered the league one season earlier than Allen, and they played together through 1990. Brown led the Oilers with five interceptions in 1985 and again in 1989. Allen amassed seven interceptions and recovered five fumbles throughout his career.

SAFETIES: Keith Bostic (1983–1988) led the team in interceptions with six in 1987. He qualified for his only Pro Bowl that season. Jeff Donaldson (1984–1989) was crucial to Houston's three straight playoff appearances to end the decade. His four interceptions were a team-high mark in 1988.

PUNTER: Greg Montgomery (1988–1993) ranks fifth all-time in franchise history in punting yards (13,529) and second in gross average per punt (43.6).

PUNT RETURNER: Carl Roaches (1980–1984) returned 151 punts for 1,095 yards, which ranks third in franchise history. His average of 7.3 yards per return ranks fifth in Oilers/Titans history among players with more than 100 returns.

Drew Hill ranks second in receiving yards in franchise history.

1990

9–7

Second in AFC Central

The Oilers and head coach Jerry Glanville agreed to separate after the 1989 season. General manager Mike Holovak replaced him with Jack Pardee, who had most recently coached college football at the University of Houston. The Oilers promoted quarterbacks coach Kevin Gilbride to offensive coordinator.

Pardee and Gilbride transitioned to a "Run & Shoot" offense. It utilized a formation consisting of four wide receivers, without a tight end or fullback. Running back Alonzo Highsmith, deemed a poor fit for the offense, was traded to the Dallas Cowboys.

Quarterback Warren Moon thrived in the aggressive system, throwing for a club-record 4,689 yards, highlighted by a 527-yard showing against the Kansas City Chiefs—the second most passing yards in a game in NFL history. Moon became the franchise's all-time leader in passing yards during the season, bringing his regular-season total to 22,989 yards. Wide receivers Haywood Jeffires (1,048) and Drew Hill (1,019) surpassed 1,000 receiving yards. Ernest Givins (979), who led the team with nine receiving touchdowns, came close to joining them.

The offense scored 405 points, the second most in franchise history. They set a team record in a blowout win over the Cleveland Browns by scoring 58 points.

First-year defensive coordinator Jim Eddy switched the defensive alignment from a 3-4 base to a 4-3. Players like Richard Johnson and Sean Jones thrived in the new look. Johnson had a career-high and team-leading eight interceptions, and Jones led the team in sacks with 12.5.

The Oilers rode their success to a 9–7 record and a wild-card berth. However, Moon suffered a dislocated thumb late in the season. In the playoffs, reserve quarterback Cody Carlson completed less than 50% of his passes and was intercepted once in a 41–14 loss to the Cincinnati Bengals.

Moon's terrific 1990 season was rewarded. He was named the Associated Press NFL Offensive Player of the Year.

Schedule

	OPPONENT	SCORE	RECORD
L	@ Atlanta Falcons	27–47	0–1
L	@ Pittsburgh Steelers	9–20	0–2
W	Indianapolis Colts	24–10	1–2
W	@ San Diego Chargers	17–7	2–2
L	San Francisco 49ers	21–24	2–3
W	Cincinnati Bengals	48–17	3–3
W	New Orleans Saints	23–10	4–3
L	New York Jets	12–17	4–4
L	@ Los Angeles Rams	13–17	4–5
W	@ Cleveland Browns	35–23	5–5
W	Buffalo Bills	27–24	6–5
L	@ Seattle Seahawks (OT)	10–13	6–6
W	Cleveland Browns	58–14	7–6
W	@ Kansas City Chiefs	27–10	8–6
L	@ Cincinnati Bengals	20–40	8–7
W	Pittsburgh Steelers	34–14	9–7
L	*@ Cincinnati Bengals*	*14–41*	*0–1*

Season Leaders

CATEGORY	TOTAL	PLAYER
Passing Yards	4,689	Warren Moon
Rushing Yards	702	Lorenzo White
Receiving Yards	1,048	Haywood Jeffires
Receptions	74	D. Hill, H. Jeffires
Interceptions	8	Richard Johnson
Sacks	12.5	Sean Jones
Points	72	Lorenzo White

Key Additions:
Lamar Lathon (LB)

Starting Lineup

Haywood Jeffires WR
Drew Hill WR
Don Maggs LT
Mike Munchak LG
Jay Pennison C
Bruce Matthews RG
David Williams RT
Ernest Givins WR
Curtis Duncan WR
Lorenzo White RB
Warren Moon QB

CB Richard Johnson
DE Sean Jones
DT Doug Smith
DT Ray Childress
DE William Fuller
CB Cris Dishman
LB Johnny Meads
LB Al Smith
LB John Grimsley
SS Bubba McDowell
FS Terry Kinard

K Teddy Garcia
KR Gerald McNeil
P Greg Montgomery
PR Gerald McNeil

Titans Trivia

Haywood Jeffires and Drew Hill became the third Oilers duo to each surpass 1,000 receiving yards in a single season.

Pro Bowl Selections

- Ray Childress (DT)
- Ernest Givins (WR)
- Drew Hill (WR)
- Bruce Matthews (G)
- Warren Moon (QB)
- Mike Munchak (G)

Warren Moon

Canadian Football League (CFL) quarterback Warren Moon made the jump to the NFL after winning five consecutive Grey Cups between 1978 and 1982.

Moon didn't begin experiencing legitimate NFL success until 1987. He threw for 21 touchdowns that season, and the Oilers fielded a top-10 scoring offense. They clinched their first postseason berth since 1980.

In 1990, Moon quarterbacked the revolutionary Run & Shoot offense, which featured four wide receivers on the field in lieu of a tight end or fullback. Moon threw for 4,689 yards and 33 touchdowns en route to NFL Offensive Player of the Year honors. His success continued in 1991, when Moon threw for a career-high and franchise-best 4,690 yards. The star quarterback still holds franchise records in several categories, including total passing yards and total passing touchdowns.

In 2006, Moon became the first African American quarterback and the first undrafted quarterback to be inducted into the Pro Football Hall of Fame. He is the only player in both the Canadian Football Hall of Fame and the Pro Football Hall of Fame.

Warren Moon led the NFL in passing yards in 1990 and 1991. He also rushed for 1,736 yards in his career.

1991

11–5
First in AFC Central

The success of the Run & Shoot offense continued in 1991. The Oilers averaged 24.1 points per game, fourth best in the league. They scored 30 or more points on five occasions, including a 47–17 Week 1 drubbing of the Los Angeles Raiders.

Quarterback Warren Moon threw for a career-high and franchise-best 4,690 yards, surpassing his personal record set during the previous season by one yard. Wide receiver Haywood Jeffires led the league with 100 receptions. He became the second player in franchise history to catch 100-plus passes in a single season. Drew Hill added 90 receptions of his own as Moon set an NFL record with 655 passing attempts.

The defense, which allowed a sixth-ranked 15.7 points per game, took another step forward under defensive coordinator Jim Eddy. Defensive end William Fuller led the AFC with 15 sacks.

With Jack Pardee's explosive offense and Eddy's stifling defense, the Oilers cruised to an 11–5 record. It represented their best regular-season record since 1980. The Oilers won their first division title since the merger, having last captured the division way back in 1967.

Houston hosted a wild-card game and defeated the New York Jets, 17–10. Safety Bubba McDowell intercepted two passes, while Ernest Givins caught both Oilers touchdowns.

Houston traveled to Denver for the divisional round. The Oilers jumped to a 14–0 lead in the first quarter. Trailing by two scores in the fourth quarter, the Broncos put a touchdown on the board, cutting Houston's lead to one point. Then quarterback John Elway led a drive that culminated in the final seconds with a game-winning field goal. The Oilers lost, 26–24.

Pro Bowl Selections

- Ray Childress (DT)
- Cris Dishman (CB)
- William Fuller (DE)
- Haywood Jeffires (WR)
- Bruce Matthews (C)
- Warren Moon (QB)
- Mike Munchak (G)
- Al Smith (LB)

Schedule

	OPPONENT	SCORE	RECORD
W	Los Angeles Raiders	47–17	1–0
W	@ Cincinnati Bengals	30–7	2–0
W	Kansas City Chiefs	17–7	3–0
L	@ New England Patriots	20–24	3–1
W	Denver Broncos	42–14	4–1
W	@ New York Jets	23–20	5–1
W	@ Miami Dolphins	17–13	6–1
W	Cincinnati Bengals	35–3	7–1
L	@ Washington (OT)	13–16	7–2
W	Dallas Cowboys (OT)	26–23	8–2
W	Cleveland Browns	28–24	9–2
L	@ Pittsburgh Steelers	14–26	9–3
L	Philadelphia Eagles	6–13	9–4
W	Pittsburgh Steelers	31–6	10–4
W	@ Cleveland Browns	17–14	11–4
L	@ New York Giants	20–24	11–5
W	*New York Jets*	*17–10*	*1–0*
L	*@ Denver Broncos*	*24–26*	*1–1*

Season Leaders

CATEGORY	TOTAL	PLAYER
Passing Yards	4,690	Warren Moon
Rushing Yards	720	Allen Pinkett
Receiving Yards	1,181	Haywood Jeffires
Receptions	100	Haywood Jeffires
Interceptions	6	Cris Dishman
Sacks	15	William Fuller
Points	64	Ian Howfield

Key Additions:
Al Del Greco (K), Darryll Lewis (CB), Marcus Robertson (FS)

Haywood Jeffires was named to the Pro Bowl 1991–1993.

Starting Lineup

OFFENSE	POSITION
Warren Moon	QB
Allen Pinkett	RB
Haywood Jeffires	WR
Drew Hill	WR
Ernest Givins	WR
Curtis Duncan	WR
Don Maggs	LT
Mike Munchak	LG
Bruce Matthews	C
Doug Dawson	RG
David Williams	RT

DEFENSE	POSITION
William Fuller	DE
Ray Childress	DT
Doug Smith	DT
Sean Jones	DE
Lamar Lathon	OLB
Al Smith	MLB
Johnny Meads	OLB
Cris Dishman	CB
Richard Johnson	CB
Bubba McDowell	SS
Bo Orlando	FS

SPECIAL TEAMS	POSITION
Ian Howfield	K
Allen Pinkett	KR
Greg Montgomery	P
Pat Coleman	PR

1992

10–6

Second in AFC Central

Several personnel-based decisions helped shape the 1992 campaign. Warren Moon signed a multi-year extension, while star wide receiver Drew Hill departed in free agency. The Oilers committed to Lorenzo White as their lead back, so Allen Pinkett was traded to New Orleans. White responded to an increased workload by rushing for a career-best 1,226 yards.

Moon threw five touchdown passes in a win over the Cincinnati Bengals, surpassing the great George Blanda to become Houston's all-time passing touchdowns leader. Haywood Jeffires caught three touchdowns in the 38–24 triumph, tying a single-game franchise record.

Unfortunately, Moon suffered multiple injuries throughout the season. While playing through a concussion, he fractured his arm in a victory over the Minnesota Vikings. Reserve quarterback Cody Carlson started Houston's final six regular-season games, leading them to four victories. The 10–6 Oilers qualified for the postseason as a wild card.

Moon returned to Houston's lineup for their first playoff game, a road date with the Buffalo Bills. That's when one of the worst moments in franchise history occurred. Four first-half touchdown passes had the Oilers holding a comfortable 28–3 halftime lead. A 58-yard pick-six in the third quarter by safety Bubba McDowell increased Houston's lead to 35–3 and should have crushed the Bills' spirits. But this was a Buffalo team in the midst of a run to four straight Super Bowls. They unfathomably scored five unanswered touchdowns—including four via scoring passes by backup quarterback Frank Reich—to take a 38–35 lead. A field goal by Al Del Greco sent the instant classic to overtime, where the Bills kicked a 32-yard game-winning field goal to complete what became known nationally as "The Comeback." The 32-point comeback still represents the largest in postseason history.

The disastrous defeat overshadowed yet another fantastic season for the Oilers. It was Houston's sixth consecutive postseason berth. A league-high nine Oilers were voted to the Pro Bowl. Nevertheless, defensive coordinator Jim Eddy was replaced by Buddy Ryan, who had famously served as the defensive coordinator of the 1985 Chicago Bears.

Schedule

	OPPONENT	SCORE	RECORD
L	Pittsburgh Steelers	24–29	0–1
W	@ Indianapolis Colts	20–10	1–1
W	Kansas City Chiefs (OT)	23–20	2–1
W	San Diego Chargers	27–0	3–1
W	@ Cincinnati Bengals	38–24	4–1
L	@ Denver Broncos	21–27	4–2
W	Cincinnati Bengals	26–10	5–2
L	@ Pittsburgh Steelers	20–21	5–3
L	Cleveland Browns	14–24	5–4
W	@ Minnesota Vikings	17–13	6–4
L	@ Miami Dolphins	16–19	6–5
W	@ Detroit Lions	24–21	7–5
W	Chicago Bears	24–7	8–5
L	Green Bay Packers	14–16	8–6
W	@ Cleveland Browns	17–14	9–6
W	Buffalo Bills	27–3	10–6
L	*Buffalo Bills (OT)*	*38–41*	*0–1*

Season Leaders

CATEGORY	TOTAL	PLAYER
Passing Yards	2,521	Warren Moon
Rushing Yards	1,226	Lorenzo White
Receiving Yards	954	Curtis Duncan
Receptions	90	Haywood Jeffires
Interceptions	6	Jerry Gray
Sacks	13	Ray Childress
Points	104	Al Del Greco

Key Additions:
Joe Bowden (LB), Eddie Robinson (LB), Webster Slaughter (WR)

Starting Lineup

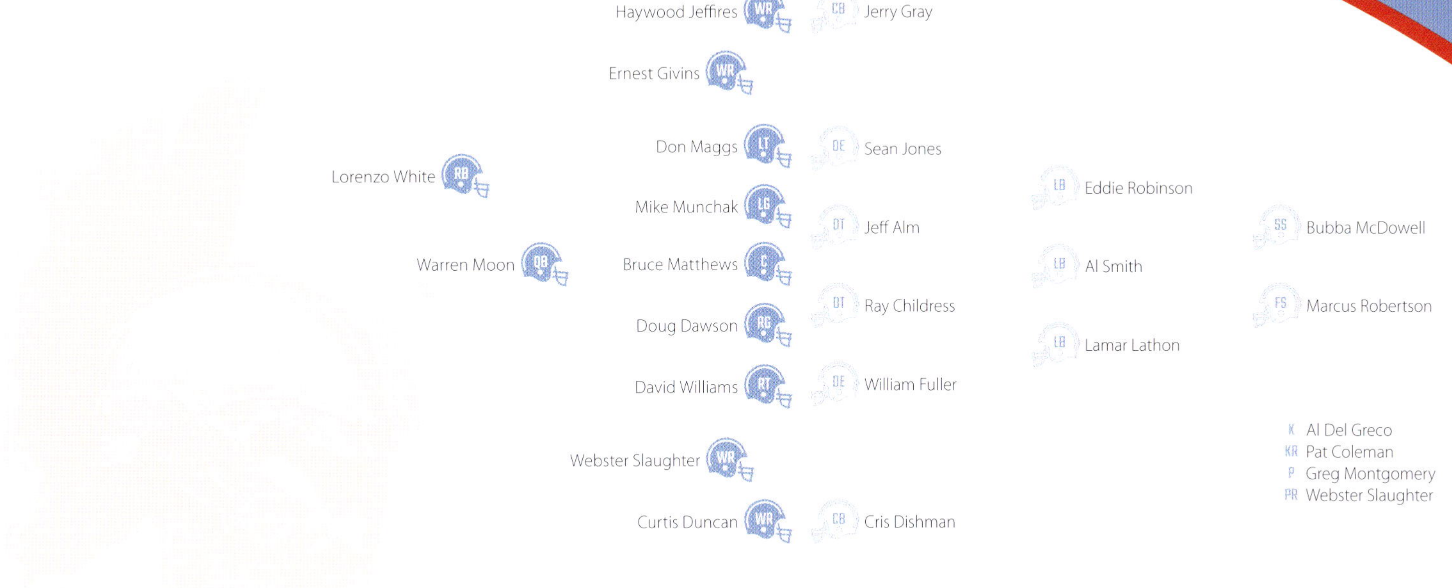

Titans Trivia

An NFL-record three wide receivers from one team were named to the Pro Bowl: Curtis Duncan, Ernest Givins, and Haywood Jeffries.

Pro Bowl Selections

- Ray Childress (DT)
- Curtis Duncan (WR)
- Ernest Givins (WR)
- Haywood Jeffries (WR)
- Bruce Matthews (C)
- Warren Moon (QB)
- Mike Munchak (G)
- Al Smith (LB)
- Lorenzo White (RB)

1993

12–4
First in AFC Central

Pressure mounted as owner Bud Adams reportedly threatened to break up the roster if the Oilers didn't reach the Super Bowl. The team responded in lackluster fashion, going 1–4 to start the season. Quarterback Warren Moon was temporarily benched after throwing 11 interceptions in that span.

Moon quickly reclaimed his starting role. Buddy Ryan's "46" defense, a run-stopping scheme that forced offenses to pass the ball, began firing on all cylinders. The Oilers rolled to 11 consecutive victories, averaging 25.5 points per game while holding their opponents to an average of 11.3 points.

Running back Lorenzo White missed time due to injury, and Gary Brown cemented his role as the lead back in his first and second starts, rushing for 166 and 194 yards respectively. He finished with 1,002 yards on the season even though his first carry didn't come until the seventh game.

The Oilers' 12 wins represented a franchise best. They won the AFC Central for the second time in three seasons and advanced to the playoffs for the seventh consecutive season—an all-time franchise best.

Houston earned a first-round bye as the AFC's second seed. However, despite defeating the Kansas City Chiefs, 30–0, during the regular season, the Oilers fell to them in the divisional round, 28–20. The Chiefs outscored Houston, 21–10, in a decisive fourth quarter.

It was a tumultuous campaign. Defensive tackle Jeff Alm tragically died by suicide during the season, following his involvement in a high-speed car crash that claimed the life of a friend. Ryan and offensive coordinator Kevin Gilbride did not get along, which many felt affected the team's chemistry. In a Super-Bowl-or-bust season, sweeping changes were on the horizon.

Pro Bowl Selections

- Ray Childress (DT)
- Haywood Jeffires (WR)
- Sean Jones (DE)
- Bruce Matthews (C)
- Greg Montgomery (P)
- Warren Moon (QB)
- Mike Munchak (G)
- Webster Slaughter (WR)

Schedule

	OPPONENT	SCORE	RECORD
L	@ New Orleans Saints	21–33	0–1
W	Kansas City Chiefs	30–0	1–1
L	@ San Diego Chargers	17–18	1–2
L	Los Angeles Rams	13–28	1–3
L	@ Buffalo Bills	7–35	1–4
W	@ New England Patriots	28–14	2–4
W	Cincinnati Bengals	28–12	3–4
W	Seattle Seahawks	24–14	4–4
W	@ Cincinnati Bengals	38–3	5–4
W	@ Cleveland Browns	27–20	6–4
W	Pittsburgh Steelers	23–3	7–4
W	Atlanta Falcons	33–17	8–4
W	Cleveland Browns	19–17	9–4
W	@ Pittsburgh Steelers	26–17	10–4
W	@ San Francisco 49ers	10–7	11–4
W	New York Jets	24–0	12–4
L	*Kansas City Chiefs*	*20–28*	*0–1*

Season Leaders

CATEGORY	TOTAL	PLAYER
Passing Yards	3,485	Warren Moon
Rushing Yards	1,002	Gary Brown
Receiving Yards	904	Webster Slaughter
Receptions	77	Webster Slaughter
Interceptions	7	Marcus Robertson
Sacks	13	Sean Jones
Points	126	Al Del Greco

Key Additions:
Blaine Bishop (S), Brad Hopkins (OT)

William Fuller started 87 games in eight seasons with the Oilers.

Starting Lineup

OFFENSE	POSITION
Warren Moon	QB
Gary Brown	RB
Haywood Jeffires	WR
Webster Slaughter	WR
Ernest Givins	WR
Curtis Duncan	WR
Brad Hopkins	LT
Mike Munchak	LG
Bruce Matthews	C
Doug Dawson	RG
David Williams	RT

DEFENSE	POSITION
William Fuller	DE
Ray Childress	DT
Glenn Montgomery	DT
Sean Jones	DE
Eddie Robinson	OLB
Al Smith	MLB
Wilber Marshall	OLB
Cris Dishman	CB
Steve Jackson	CB
Bubba McDowell	SS
Marcus Robertson	FS

SPECIAL TEAMS	POSITION
Al Del Greco	K
Willie Drewrey	KR
Greg Montgomery	P
Willie Drewrey	PR

1994

2–14

Fourth in AFC Central

Owner Bud Adams delivered on rumors of sweeping changes following the Oilers' latest postseason failure. After the league agreed to implement a salary cap, limiting a team's spending on player salaries, quarterback Warren Moon was traded to the Minnesota Vikings, signaling that a rebuild had begun.

Cost-cutting efforts profoundly impacted the team's roster. Defensive ends William Fuller and Sean Jones were lost to unrestricted free agency, as was punter Greg Montgomery.

Defensive coordinator Buddy Ryan left to become head coach of the Arizona Cardinals. He was replaced by Jeff Fisher. General manager Mike Holovak became vice president of player personnel and scouting. Assistant general manager Floyd Reese was selected as the new general manager.

Left guard Mike Munchak announced his retirement ahead of the 1994 campaign. His number 63 was retired during the season, and he was later inducted into the Pro Football Hall of Fame in 2001.

Cody Carlson was named the starting quarterback, but he was routinely in and out of the lineup due to injuries. Third-year quarterback Bucky Richardson was next in line, but he was eventually replaced due to ineffectiveness. Free agent Billy Joe Tolliver ended up starting a team-high seven games at quarterback. The Oilers lost all seven of his starts. Houston's offense was abysmal, scoring a league-low 14.1 points per game.

Head coach Jack Pardee and offensive coordinator Kevin Gilbride were relieved of their duties following a 1–9 start. Fisher was named head coach, and he maintained control of the defense. Gilbride's firing led to the dismantling of the Oilers' infamous Run & Shoot offense.

Ernest Givins became the Oilers' all-time leader in receiving yards with 7,935. He surpassed Drew Hill (7,447).

Pro Bowl Selections

- Bruce Matthews (C)

Schedule

	OPPONENT	SCORE	RECORD
L	@ Indianapolis Colts	21–45	0–1
L	@ Dallas Cowboys	17–20	0–2
L	Buffalo Bills	7–15	0–3
W	Cincinnati Bengals	20–13	1–3
L	@ Pittsburgh Steelers	14–30	1–4
L	Cleveland Browns	8–11	1–5
L	@ Philadelphia Eagles	6–21	1–6
L	@ Los Angeles Raiders	14–17	1–7
L	Pittsburgh Steelers (OT)	9–12	1–8
L	@ Cincinnati Bengals	31–34	1–9
L	New York Giants	10–13	1–10
L	@ Cleveland Browns	10–34	1–11
L	Arizona Cardinals	12–30	1–12
L	Seattle Seahawks	14–16	1–13
L	@ Kansas City Chiefs	9–31	1–14
W	New York Jets	24–10	2–14

Season Leaders

CATEGORY	TOTAL	PLAYER
Passing Yards	1,287	Billy Joe Tolliver
Rushing Yards	757	Lorenzo White
Receiving Yards	846	Webster Slaughter
Receptions	68	H. Jeffires, W. Slaughter
Interceptions	5	Darryll Lewis
Sacks	8.5	Lamar Lathon
Points	66	Al Del Greco

Key Additions:
Henry Ford (DE)

Cris Dishman intercepted 31 passes in nine years with the Oilers.

Starting Lineup

OFFENSE	POSITION
Billy Joe Tolliver	QB
Lorenzo White	RB
Gary Brown	RB
Webster Slaughter	WR
Haywood Jeffires	WR
Pat Carter	TE
Brad Hopkins	LT
John Flannery	LG
Bruce Matthews	C
Kevin Donnalley	RG
David Williams	RT

DEFENSE	POSITION
Kenny Davidson	DE
Ray Childress	DT
Glenn Montgomery	DT
Lamar Lathon	DE
Eddie Robinson	OLB
Al Smith	MLB
Micheal Barrow	OLB
Cris Dishman	CB
Darryll Lewis	CB
Blaine Bishop	SS
Marcus Robertson	FS

SPECIAL TEAMS	POSITION
Al Del Greco	K
Todd McNair	KR
Rich Camarillo	P
Ernest Givins	PR

1995

7–9

Second in AFC Central

Owner Bud Adams confirmed that Jeff Fisher would remain the Oilers head coach. Fisher named Jerry Rhome his offensive coordinator and Steve Sidwell his defensive coordinator. Retired guard Mike Munchak joined the staff as an offensive assistant.

The NFL added two teams to the league: the Carolina Panthers and the Jacksonville Jaguars. The Jaguars joined the Oilers in the AFC Central, bringing the number of teams within that division to five.

With the third overall pick in the 1995 NFL Draft, general manager Floyd Reese selected quarterback Steve McNair. The Oilers needed a long-term solution at the position, despite signing veteran free agent Chris Chandler.

McNair began the season as Chandler's backup and only saw action in four games. McNair started two of those games, and the Oilers won both of them. The team also received immediate contributions from various rookies. Wide receiver Chris Sanders led the team in receiving yards (823) and touchdowns (9). Sanders helped replace Ernest Givins, who joined the expansion Jaguars. Running back Rodney Thomas rushed for 947 yards and five touchdowns. Defensive tackle Gary Walker joined Sanders on the NFL All-Rookie Team.

Pro Bowl center Mark Stepnoski was signed as a free agent, which allowed Bruce Matthews to shift from center to left guard. The Oilers claimed tight end Frank Wycheck off waivers. He would quickly develop into a cornerstone offensive piece.

The season was overshadowed by bombshell reports that surfaced in August. Owner Bud Adams was looking at options for relocating the franchise to Nashville, Tennessee. Adams had been displeased with matters surrounding the Houston Astrodome since 1993 and was involved in a lengthy financial-related standoff with its parent company. Adams' lease with the Astrodome was set to expire at the conclusion of 1997.

On November 17, Adams and Nashville mayor Phil Bredesen signed an agreement to begin the process of moving the Oilers to Nashville.

Schedule

	OPPONENT	SCORE	RECORD
W	@ Jacksonville Jaguars	10–3	1–0
L	Pittsburgh Steelers	17–34	1–1
L	Cleveland Browns	7–14	1–2
W	@ Cincinnati Bengals	38–28	2–2
L	Jacksonville Jaguars	16–17	2–3
L	@ Minnesota Vikings (OT)	17–23	2–4
L	@ Chicago Bears	32–35	2–5
W	Tampa Bay Buccaneers	19–7	3–5
W	@ Cleveland Browns	37–10	4–5
L	Cincinnati Bengals	25–32	4–6
L	@ Kansas City Chiefs	13–20	4–7
W	Denver Broncos	42–33	5–7
L	@ Pittsburgh Steelers	7–21	5–8
L	Detroit Lions	17–24	5–9
W	New York Jets	23–6	6–9
W	@ Buffalo Bills	28–17	7–9

Season Leaders

CATEGORY	TOTAL	PLAYER
Passing Yards	2,460	Chris Chandler
Rushing Yards	947	Rodney Thomas
Receiving Yards	823	Chris Sanders
Receptions	61	Haywood Jeffires
Interceptions	6	Darryll Lewis
Sacks	4.5	A. Cook, H. Ford
Points	114	Al Del Greco

Key Additions:
Steve McNair (QB), Mark Stepnoski (C), Gary Walker (DT), Frank Wycheck (TE)

Starting Lineup

Titans Trivia

Frank Wycheck had just 168 receiving yards in two seasons with Washington. He was released, allowing Houston to claim him.

Pro Bowl Selections

- Blaine Bishop (S)
- Darryll Lewis (CB)
- Bruce Matthews (G)
- Mark Stepnoski (C)

The Move to Tennessee

Dissatisfied with the state of his stadium in Houston, Bud Adams signed an agreement with Nashville mayor Phil Bredesen in 1995, which awarded Nashville a negotiating period to commit to building a stadium for Adams' franchise. In November of 1995, Adams and Bredesen signed an agreement to begin the process of moving the Oilers to Nashville.

The move from Houston to Nashville earned majority approval by NFL team owners in April of 1996. A week later, voters in Davidson County approved a referendum that offered public support and funding to build a stadium in downtown Nashville.

The Oilers fan base was furious. Support for the team waned so much that Adams was forced to end his lease with the Astrodome after the 1996 season—a year earlier than originally planned. With Nashville's downtown stadium not yet finished for Adams' accelerated timeline, the franchise played its 1997 home games at the Liberty Bowl Memorial Stadium in Memphis, Tennessee, under the Tennessee Oilers moniker.

Memphis showed little support for the Oilers, prompting Adams to move the team again for the 1998 season, this time to Vanderbilt Stadium in Nashville. On November 14, 1998, Adams announced the franchise would be renamed the Tennessee Titans.

In 1999, construction was finalized on the new state-of-the-art stadium. In July, it was officially unveiled as Adelphia Coliseum. After enduring years of headaches and hurdles, the Titans moved into their full-time home for what proved to be a magical 1999 season.

Bud Adams (right) presents Nashville mayor Phil Bredesen with a personalized Oilers jersey.

BREDESEN
1

1996

8–8
Fourth in AFC Central

In April, NFL team owners approved the Houston Oilers' relocation to Nashville, Tennessee. Division rivals the Cincinnati Bengals and Pittsburgh Steelers were among those that voted against the move. A week later, voters in Davidson County, Tennessee, approved a referendum that offered public funding to build a stadium in downtown Nashville.

That wasn't the only shake-up in the AFC Central. The Cleveland Browns moved, becoming the Baltimore Ravens.

Two stellar players departed the Oilers in wide receiver Haywood Jeffires and defensive lineman Ray Childress. In nine seasons with the Oilers, Jeffires recorded 515 receptions for 6,119 yards and 47 touchdowns. He is second on the franchise's all-time leader board in receptions, is fifth in receiving yards, and is tied for second in receiving touchdowns. Childress totaled 75.5 sacks, thriving both as a defensive end and defensive tackle—based on team needs. He qualified for five Pro Bowls and served as a captain in nine of 11 seasons. He was the ultimate team player.

The Oilers executed two trades in Round 1 of the 1996 NFL draft and landed at the 14th overall selection. They used the pick on running back Eddie George, who proved to be a brilliant selection. George rushed for 1,368 yards and eight touchdowns as a rookie. His efforts were rewarded with NFL Offensive Rookie of the Year honors.

Chris Chandler remained the Oilers starting quarterback. Steve McNair started four games and continued to flash promise by throwing for six touchdowns. A dual-threat quarterback, he added 169 rushing yards and two additional touchdowns to his offensive totals.

Public support for the Oilers plummeted in Houston. The fan base showed little interest in supporting a franchise that was leaving them. The Oilers averaged 31,825 fans per home game, their second-lowest total since the 1970 AFL-NFL merger. They posted a lackluster 2–6 record at home, while they were 6–2 on the road. Everything transpiring off the field was clearly a distraction.

Schedule

	OPPONENT	SCORE	RECORD
L	Kansas City Chiefs	19–20	0–1
W	@ Jacksonville Jaguars	34–27	1–1
W	Baltimore Ravens	29–13	2–1
L	@ Pittsburgh Steelers	16–30	2–2
W	@ Cincinnati Bengals (OT)	30–27	3–2
W	@ Atlanta Falcons	23–13	4–2
W	Pittsburgh Steelers	23–13	5–2
L	San Francisco 49ers	9–10	5–3
L	@ Seattle Seahawks	16–23	5–4
W	@ New Orleans Saints	31–14	6–4
L	Miami Dolphins	20–23	6–5
L	Carolina Panthers	6–31	6–6
W	@ New York Jets	35–10	7–6
L	Jacksonville Jaguars	17–23	7–7
L	Cincinnati Bengals	13–21	7–8
W	@ Baltimore Ravens	24–21	8–8

Season Leaders

CATEGORY	TOTAL	PLAYER
Passing Yards	2,099	Chris Chandler
Rushing Yards	1,368	Eddie George
Receiving Yards	882	Chris Sanders
Receptions	53	Frank Wycheck
Interceptions	5	Darryll Lewis
Sacks	7.5	Anthony Cook
Points	131	Al Del Greco

Key Additions:
Eddie George (RB), Jon Runyan (OT)

Starting Lineup

Titans Trivia

Al Del Greco became the franchise's all-time career field goals leader in 1996, surpassing Tony Zendejas.

Pro Bowl Selections

- Blaine Bishop (S)
- Bruce Matthews (G)
- John Henry Mills (ST)
- Mark Stepnoski (C)

1997

8–8

Third in AFC Central

After the lack of support for the Oilers in 1996, owner Bud Adams reached an agreement to end his lease with the Houston Astrodome a year early. Nashville's downtown stadium was not yet completed, so the franchise played its 1997 home games as the Tennessee Oilers at the Liberty Bowl Memorial Stadium in Memphis, Tennessee.

Defensive coordinator Steve Sidwell was replaced by Gregg Williams, and offensive coordinator Jerry Rhome was also let go. Rhome was succeeded by Les Steckel, who received an in-house promotion from wide receivers coach. Mike Munchak was promoted to offensive line coach.

With third-year quarterback Steve McNair ready to step into the starting role, general manager Floyd Reese traded veteran Chris Chandler to the Atlanta Falcons. The move to Tennessee felt like appropriate timing for the franchise to begin anew at quarterback. McNair started all 16 games, throwing for 2,665 yards and 14 touchdowns. He also rushed for 674 yards and a team-high eight touchdowns, even outpacing Eddie George in the latter category. George rushed for 1,399 yards and six touchdowns on the way to his first Pro Bowl.

First-round draft pick Kenny Holmes tied for the team lead in sacks as a rookie with seven. Tight end Frank Wycheck developed into a dynamic weapon by leading the offense in receptions (63), receiving yards (748), and receiving touchdowns (4). With one of the draft picks acquired in the Chandler deal with Atlanta, the Oilers selected wide receiver Derrick Mason, whose time as a game-changer on offense would soon arrive.

The Oilers won their inaugural game in Tennessee, defeating the Oakland Raiders, 24–21, in overtime. George tied a franchise record by rushing for 216 yards in the game.

Despite fielding an exciting offense filled with young playmakers and a stingy defense, even fewer fans attended home games in Memphis compared to the previous year in Houston. Local fans were disinterested in supporting a franchise they'd soon lose to Nashville.

Schedule

	OPPONENT	SCORE	RECORD
W	Oakland Raiders (OT)	24–21	1–0
L	@ Miami Dolphins (OT)	13–16	1–1
L	Baltimore Ravens	10–36	1–2
L	@ Pittsburgh Steelers	24–37	1–3
L	@ Seattle Seahawks	13–16	1–4
W	Cincinnati Bengals	30–7	2–4
W	Washington	28–14	3–4
W	@ Arizona Cardinals	41–14	4–4
L	Jacksonville Jaguars	24–30	4–5
W	New York Giants	10–6	5–5
L	@ Jacksonville Jaguars	9–17	5–6
W	Buffalo Bills	31–14	6–6
W	@ Dallas Cowboys	27–14	7–6
L	@ Cincinnati Bengals	14–41	7–7
L	@ Baltimore Ravens	19–21	7–8
W	Pittsburgh Steelers	16–6	8–8

Season Leaders

CATEGORY	TOTAL	PLAYER
Passing Yards	2,665	Steve McNair
Rushing Yards	1,399	Eddie George
Receiving Yards	748	Frank Wycheck
Receptions	63	Frank Wycheck
Interceptions	5	D. Lewis, M. Robertson
Sacks	7	K. Holmes, G. Walker
Points	113	Al Del Greco

Key Additions:

Kenny Holmes (DE), Derrick Mason (WR), Denard Walker (CB)

Starting Lineup

Titans Trivia

The trade with Atlanta was a win-win. Both teams advanced to a Super Bowl with their new starting quarterbacks.

Pro Bowl Selections

- Blaine Bishop (S)
- Eddie George (RB)
- Bruce Matthews (G)

1998

8–8

Second in AFC Central

Due to lackluster attendance numbers in Memphis, the Tennessee Oilers found themselves on the move for a second season in a row. A local solution in Nashville was identified: The Oilers would play their home games at Vanderbilt Stadium. The move improved attendance by nearly 10,000 fans per game, as an average of 37,444 fans attended home games in 1998.

On July 29, owner Bud Adams announced that the franchise would adopt a new moniker for the 1999 season. The team's new name was revealed in November: the Tennessee Titans. A nod to Greek mythology, the name paid tribute to Nashville's reputation as the "Athens of the South."

General manager Floyd Reese selected wide receiver Kevin Dyson with the 16th pick in the 1998 NFL Draft. (Just five picks later, the Minnesota Vikings selected wide receiver Randy Moss, who would develop into one of the greatest receivers of all time.) Reese added cornerback Samari Rolle in the second round and guard Benji Olson in the fifth round. Punter Craig Hentrich was added via free agency. His debut season in Tennessee saw him average a league-high 47.2 yards per punt.

In Week 2, the Oilers scored their first touchdown in Nashville when quarterback Steve McNair threw a 15-yard score to tight end Frank Wycheck. Unfortunately, the Oilers didn't win their first game in Nashville until Week 7, when they routed the Cincinnati Bengals, 44–14.

Owning a record of 8–6 late in the season, the Oilers were in position to qualify for the playoffs. However, Jeff Fisher's squad ended the season with back-to-back losses.

Days before the regular-season finale, Adams revealed the Titans logo and colors. The "Oilers" era officially ended with a 26–16 loss to the Vikings.

Schedule

	OPPONENT	SCORE	RECORD
W	@ Cincinnati Bengals	23–14	1–0
L	San Diego Chargers	7–13	1–1
L	@ New England Patriots	16–27	1–2
L	Jacksonville Jaguars	22–27	1–3
W	@ Baltimore Ravens	12–8	2–3
W	Cincinnati Bengals	44–14	3–3
L	Chicago Bears	20–23	3–4
W	@ Pittsburgh Steelers	41–31	4–4
W	@ Tampa Bay Buccaneers	31–22	5–4
W	Pittsburgh Steelers	23–14	6–4
L	New York Jets	3–24	6–5
L	@ Seattle Seahawks	18–20	6–6
W	Baltimore Ravens	16–14	7–6
W	@ Jacksonville Jaguars	16–13	8–6
L	@ Green Bay Packers	22–30	8–7
L	Minnesota Vikings	16–26	8–8

Season Leaders

CATEGORY	TOTAL	PLAYER
Passing Yards	3,228	Steve McNair
Rushing Yards	1,294	Eddie George
Receiving Yards	768	Frank Wycheck
Receptions	70	Frank Wycheck
Interceptions	4	Darryll Lewis
Sacks	4	Lonnie Marts
Points	136	Al Del Greco

Pro Bowl Selections

- Eddie George (RB)
- Craig Hentrich (P)
- Bruce Matthews (G)
- Frank Wycheck (TE)

Key Additions:
Kevin Dyson (WR), Craig Hentrich (P), Benji Olson (G), Samari Rolle (CB)

Starting Lineup

OFFENSE	POSITION
Steve McNair	QB
Eddie George	RB
Yancey Thigpen	WR
Willie Davis	WR
Jackie Harris	TE
Frank Wycheck	TE
Brad Hopkins	LT
Bruce Matthews	LG
Mark Stepnoski	C
Jason Layman	RG
Jon Runyan	RT

DEFENSE	POSITION
Pratt Lyons	DE
Gary Walker	DT
Josh Evans	DT
Kenny Holmes	DE
Eddie Robinson	OLB
Joe Bowden	MLB
Lonnie Marts	OLB
Denard Walker	CB
Darryll Lewis	CB
Blaine Bishop	SS
Marcus Robertson	FS

SPECIAL TEAMS	POSITION
Al Del Greco	K
Mike Archie	KR
Craig Hentrich	P
Derrick Mason	PR

Frank Wycheck gained more than 500 receiving yards in every season from 1996 to 2001.

1999

13–3

Second in AFC Central, AFC Champions

The Tennessee Titans moved into their new stadium, which was officially unveiled in July as Adelphia Coliseum. Head coach Jeff Fisher hired Jim Schwartz as a defensive assistant, and Jim Washburn was named defensive line coach. Both would spend several successful years with the franchise.

In the 1999 NFL Draft, general manager Floyd Reese selected Jevon Kearse, a defensive end who exploded as a rookie. He set an NFL rookie record with 14.5 sacks en route to Defensive Rookie of the Year honors. Kearse also became the first rookie to start at defensive end in a Pro Bowl since 1978.

The Titans opened the 1999 season at home and captured a thrilling, 36–35, come-from-behind victory over the Cincinnati Bengals. Quarterback Steve McNair threw for 341 yards, and kicker Al Del Greco connected on a game-winning field goal in front of 65,272 screaming Titans fans.

McNair suffered a back injury that caused him to miss the next five games. Veteran Neil O'Donnell filled in admirably and compiled a 4–1 record. When McNair returned from injury, he lifted the Titans to a 24–21 victory over the Saint Louis Rams.

The Titans dominated the regular season, finishing with a 13–3 record. Yet they were forced to settle for a wild-card berth. The Jacksonville Jaguars, whom the Titans had beaten twice—including a 41–14 statement victory at Adelphia Coliseum—captured the AFC Central Division with a 14–2 record.

The Titans hosted the Buffalo Bills in the wild-card round. The back-and-forth affair ended with the Music City Miracle—perhaps the greatest moment in franchise history. (See page 108.)

The Titans next traveled to Indianapolis for a matchup with the Colts. Eddie George rushed for 162 yards, including a go-ahead 68-yard touchdown during the third quarter. Tennessee won a hard-fought victory, 19–16.

In the AFC Championship Game, the Titans took down the Jaguars for a third time. Tennessee outscored Jacksonville 23–0 in the second half to win, 33–14, and advance to Super Bowl XXXIV, where one yard would make all the difference. (See page 108.)

Schedule

	OPPONENT	SCORE	RECORD
W	Cincinnati Bengals	36–35	1–0
W	Cleveland Browns	26–9	2–0
W	@ Jacksonville Jaguars	20–19	3–0
L	@ San Francisco 49ers	22–24	3–1
W	Baltimore Ravens	14–11	4–1
W	@ New Orleans Saints	24–21	5–1
W	Saint Louis Rams	24–21	6–1
L	@ Miami Dolphins	0–17	6–2
W	@ Cincinnati Bengals	24–14	7–2
W	Pittsburgh Steelers	26–10	8–2
W	@ Cleveland Browns	33–21	9–2
L	@ Baltimore Ravens	14–41	9–3
W	Oakland Raiders	21–14	10–3
W	Atlanta Falcons	30–17	11–3
W	Jacksonville Jaguars	41–14	12–3
W	@ Pittsburgh Steelers	47–36	13–3
W	*Buffalo Bills*	*22–16*	*1–0*
W	*@ Indianapolis Colts*	*19–16*	*2–0*
W	*@ Jacksonville Jaguars*	*33–14*	*3–0*
L	*Saint Louis Rams (@ Atlanta)*	*16–23*	*3–1*

Season Leaders

CATEGORY	TOTAL	PLAYER
Passing Yards	2,179	Steve McNair
Rushing Yards	1,304	Eddie George
Receiving Yards	658	Kevin Dyson
Receptions	69	Frank Wycheck
Interceptions	4	Samari Rolle
Sacks	14.5	Jevon Kearse
Points	106	Al Del Greco

Key Additions:
Jevon Kearse (DE), Zach Piller (G)

Starting Lineup

Titans Trivia

Owner Bud Adams unveiled the Oilers/Titans Hall of Fame in 1999, a move that signaled the past would never be forgotten.

Pro Bowl Selections

- Eddie George (RB)
- Jevon Kearse (DE)
- Bruce Matthews (G)
- Frank Wycheck (TE)

Music City Miracle

The Music City Miracle is arguably the greatest play and most famous moment in franchise history. The Titans hosted the Buffalo Bills in the wild-card round of the 1999 season. The Bills rallied in the second half to take a 13–12 lead in the fourth quarter.

A gritty drive saw the Titans recapture the upper hand via a 36-yard field goal from Al Del Greco with 1:48 remaining. The Bills used up nearly all of that time to march down the field and score a go-ahead field goal with a mere 16 seconds left in the game. Buffalo led, 16–15, so only a miracle finish could save the Titans.

That's when it happened. Fullback Lorenzo Neal fielded a pooch kickoff and immediately handed the ball to tight end Frank Wycheck. He executed the "Home Run Throwback," a play designed by special teams coordinator Alan Lowry. Wycheck threw a lateral across the field to wide receiver Kevin Dyson, who returned the kickoff 75 yards for the game-winning touchdown.

Legendary commentator Mike Keith screamed, "Touchdown, Titans! There are no flags on the field. It's a miracle. Tennessee has pulled a miracle." The play earned the nickname "Music City Miracle" and gave the franchise their first playoff win in nearly a decade.

Victories over the Indianapolis Colts and Jacksonville Jaguars propelled the Titans to Super Bowl XXXIV, the first Super Bowl appearance in franchise history. Their opponent was the Saint Louis Rams.

Tennessee's outstanding defense slowed but couldn't stop the high-powered Rams offense. Saint Louis grabbed a 16–0 advantage in the third quarter. However, the Titans began mounting a valiant come-from-behind effort.

Two Eddie George touchdowns narrowed the Rams' lead to 16–13 in the fourth quarter. Then kicker Al Del Greco connected on a 43-yard field goal to tie the game. The Rams swiftly responded with a 73-yard touchdown pass from Kurt Warner to Isaac Bruce with 1:54 remaining.

Quarterback Steve McNair led a 10-play, 87-yard drive that positioned the Titans to send the game into overtime. With six seconds left, McNair hit Dyson for a nine-yard gain, but he was tackled one yard short of the end zone as time expired. The Rams defeated the Titans, 23–16.

Music City Miracle: Kevin Dyson (87) takes a kickoff return 75 yards for a touchdown.

TITANS
35
TITANS
87

All-1990s Offense

QUARTERBACK: Choosing between Warren Moon (1984–1993) and Steve McNair in the 1990s was the most difficult All-Decade decision of this book. McNair became the starter in 1997 and led the Titans to a Super Bowl appearance. Ultimately, it was impossible to ignore Moon's individual success. He set the franchise's single-season record in passing yards twice. His 33 touchdown passes in 1990 rank second in team history.

RUNNING BACKS: Eddie George (1996–2003) ran for 1,368 yards and eight touchdowns on the way to capturing NFL Offensive Rookie of the Year honors. George rushed for more than 1,200 yards in all four of his seasons in the 1990s and was named to three Pro Bowls this decade. Lorenzo White (1988–1994) reached his performance ceiling in 1992, rushing for a career-high 1,226 yards and earning a Pro Bowl nod in the process.

WIDE RECEIVERS: Haywood Jeffires (1987–1995) enjoyed his best season in 1991, leading the league in receptions with 100. He made the Pro Bowl for three straight seasons from 1991 to 1993. Like Jeffires, Ernest Givins (1986–1994) was critical to the success of the Run & Shoot offense. He gained more than 750 receiving yards in every season between 1990 and 1993. Givins ranks first in franchise history in total receptions (542) and total receiving yards (7,935).

TIGHT END: Frank Wycheck (1995–2003) was a focal point of the Oilers/Titans passing game. He led the team in receptions from 1996 to 1999. Wycheck was named to three Pro Bowls throughout his career, and he played a key role in the Music City Miracle.

CENTER: Bruce Matthews (1983–2001) served as the team's center for four seasons in the 1990s. He started in a franchise-best 229 consecutive games, a record that will likely never be broken. Matthews never missed a game due to injury throughout his team-record 19-year career.

GUARDS: It's rare to see a position player listed at two different spots on the same All-Decade team, but Bruce Matthews (1983–2001) was that outstanding and versatile. He qualified for 14 straight Pro Bowls from 1988 to 2001. His jersey was retired by the franchise, and he became the first Tennessee Titan inducted into the hall of fame in 2007. Mike Munchak (1982–1993) enjoyed the best seasons of his hall-of-fame career during the 1980s, but he qualified for the Pro Bowl in every season he played in the 1990s. He retired after the 1993 season.

TACKLES: Brad Hopkins (1993–2005) became the starting left tackle as a rookie and maintained the position until his retirement. He ranks fourth in franchise history with 194 games played. David Williams (1989–1995) started 81 games at right tackle throughout the 1990s. He was a key member of the successful Run & Shoot offense.

KICKER: Al Del Greco (1991–2000) owns several team kicking records. His 246 field goals rank first in franchise history, as do his 1,060 career points. He scored a franchise-best 136 points in 1998.

KICK RETURNER: Mel Gray (1995–1997) arrived in free agency as a prolific kick returner with four Pro Bowl appearances. In 1995 and 1996, he accounted for 2,407 kick return yards, averaging 23.4 yards per return.

Statistics for the all-decade team are for the given decade only, unless otherwise noted.

All-1990s Defense

DEFENSIVE ENDS: William Fuller (1986–1993) recorded a career-high 15 sacks in 1991, tied for second most in the league, and was named to his first Pro Bowl. Fuller totaled 41 sacks with the Oilers in four seasons during the 1990s. Sean Jones (1988–1993) led the Oilers in sacks in 1990 with 12.5. He followed that by amassing 18.5 sacks across 1991 and 1992. Jones enjoyed his best season with the Oilers in 1993, totaling a team-high 13 sacks.

DEFENSIVE TACKLES: A dominant defensive end during the 1980s, Ray Childress (1985–1995) began playing defensive tackle in 1990 due to a schematic overhaul. He elevated his production to new heights as a defensive tackle. Childress was chosen for four consecutive Pro Bowls from 1990 to 1993. Glenn Montgomery (1989–1995) was a primary starter from 1993 to 1995. He amassed 154 tackles and 11 sacks across those seasons.

LINEBACKERS: Al Smith (1987–1996) recorded three consecutive 100-tackle seasons from 1990 to 1992. He was voted to the Pro Bowl in 1991 and 1992, and he earned First-Team All-Pro honors in 1992. Smith spent his entire 10-year career with the Oilers. Eddie Robinson (1992–1995, 1998–2001) had a career-high 90 tackles in 1998 and a personal-best six sacks in 1999, helping the Titans advance to Super Bowl XXXIV. Joe Bowden (1992–1999) developed into a full-time starter in 1995. His best season was in 1998, when he surpassed 100 tackles.

CORNERBACKS: Cris Dishman (1988–1996) developed into a ball magnet as a nine-year player for the Oilers. He led the team in interceptions in 1991 with six, earning him a Pro Bowl nod and First-Team All-Pro honors. Dishman's 31 career interceptions rank second in franchise history. From 1994 to 1998, Darryll Lewis (1991–1998) recorded 27 interceptions and led the franchise in that category for five straight seasons. He was named to his only Pro Bowl in 1995.

SAFETIES: Blaine Bishop (1993–2001) was one of the most feared defenders in the league. A four-time Pro Bowl player, Bishop racked up 697 tackles across nine seasons with the franchise. Marcus Robertson (1991–2000) intercepted a team-high seven passes in 1993 and earned First-Team All-Pro honors. He played for the Houston Oilers, Tennessee Oilers, and Tennessee Titans.

PUNTER: Greg Montgomery (1988–1993) led the league in yards per punt three times. He made the Pro Bowl and First-Team All-Pro in 1993. Montgomery ranks fifth all-time in franchise history in punting yards (13,529).

PUNT RETURNER: Mel Gray (1995–1997) averaged 10.1 yards per punt return in 1995, which is tied for 11th in a single season in franchise history (minimum 20 punt returns).

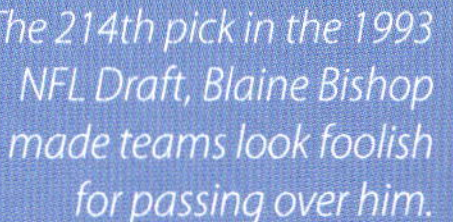

The 214th pick in the 1993 NFL Draft, Blaine Bishop made teams look foolish for passing over him.

2000

13–3
First in AFC Central

Head coach Jeff Fisher hired two-time Super Bowl winner Mike Heimerdinger to replace Les Steckel as offensive coordinator. General manager Floyd Reese drafted linebacker Keith Bulluck with the 30th pick in the 2000 NFL Draft.

The schedule-makers pitted the Titans against the Buffalo Bills in Week 1, a rematch of the famous Music City Miracle game. The Bills exacted revenge, defeating the Titans, 16–13. Tennessee responded with eight consecutive victories, highlighted by a 14–6 win over the rival Baltimore Ravens.

In a Week 11 rematch, the Ravens bested the Titans, 24–23, Tennessee's first ever loss at Adelphia Coliseum, ending a streak of 12 regular-season wins. The Titans finished 13–3 for a second straight season and won the AFC Central Division. They finished with the best record in the league, clinching a first-round bye and home-field advantage throughout the postseason.

Tennessee's divisional-round playoff opponent was the Ravens. The Titans outgained them, 317 yards to 134. They converted 23 first downs to the Ravens' six. On special teams, Titans wide receiver Chris Coleman blocked two punts. Nevertheless, the teams entered the fourth quarter in a tie game, 10–10. In disastrous fashion, a field goal by Al Del Greco that would've given Tennessee the lead was blocked and returned 90 yards for a game-changing touchdown. (Del Greco missed three of four field goal attempts in the game.) Quarterback Steve McNair mounted a potential game-tying drive, when a pass intended for Eddie George was juggled into the hands of linebacker Ray Lewis, who returned it for a touchdown. The surprising turn of events put an end to the Titans' season, 24–10.

A franchise-tying record nine players were named to the Pro Bowl.

Pro Bowl Selections

- Blaine Bishop (S)
- Eddie George (RB)
- Brad Hopkins (OT)
- Jevon Kearse (DE)
- Derrick Mason (KR)
- Bruce Matthews (G)
- Steve McNair (QB)
- Samari Rolle (CB)
- Frank Wycheck (TE)

Schedule

	OPPONENT	SCORE	RECORD
L	@ Buffalo Bills	13–16	0–1
W	Kansas City Chiefs (OT)	17–14	1–1
W	@ Pittsburgh Steelers	23–20	2–1
W	New York Giants	28–14	3–1
W	@ Cincinnati Bengals	23–14	4–1
W	Jacksonville Jaguars	27–13	5–1
W	@ Baltimore Ravens	14–6	6–1
W	@ Washington	27–21	7–1
W	Pittsburgh Steelers	9–7	8–1
L	Baltimore Ravens	23–24	8–2
W	Cleveland Browns	24–10	9–2
L	@ Jacksonville Jaguars	13–16	9–3
W	@ Philadelphia Eagles	15–13	10–3
W	Cincinnati Bengals	35–3	11–3
W	@ Cleveland Browns	24–0	12–3
W	Dallas Cowboys	31–0	13–3
L	*Baltimore Ravens*	*10–24*	*0–1*

Season Leaders

CATEGORY	TOTAL	PLAYER
Passing Yards	2,847	Steve McNair
Rushing Yards	1,509	Eddie George
Receiving Yards	895	Derrick Mason
Receptions	70	Frank Wycheck
Interceptions	7	Samari Rolle
Sacks	11.5	Jevon Kearse
Points	118	Al Del Greco

Key Additions:
Keith Bulluck (LB), Fred Miller (OT)

Starting Lineup

OFFENSE	POSITION
Steve McNair	QB
Eddie George	RB
Lorenzo Neal	RB
Chris Sanders	WR
Derrick Mason	WR
Frank Wycheck	TE
Brad Hopkins	LT
Bruce Matthews	LG
Kevin Long	C
Benji Olson	RG
Fred Miller	RT

DEFENSE	POSITION
Jevon Kearse	DE
John Thornton	DT
Jason Fisk	DT
Kenny Holmes	DE
Greg Favors	OLB
Randall Godfrey	MLB
Eddie Robinson	OLB
Denard Walker	CB
Samari Rolle	CB
Blaine Bishop	SS
Marcus Robertson	FS

SPECIAL TEAMS	POSITION
Al Del Greco	K
Derrick Mason	KR
Craig Hentrich	P
Derrick Mason	PR

"Pressure is what you make of it. It makes me play harder."
—Steve McNair

Samari Rolle was First-Team All-Pro in 2000.

2001

7–9
Fourth in AFC Central

Defensive coordinator Gregg Williams left the team to become the new head coach of the Buffalo Bills. Jeff Fisher promoted Jim Schwartz as Williams' replacement.

Starting safety Marcus Robertson departed in free agency. Rookie Andre Dyson replaced Denard Walker at cornerback. Kicker Joe Nedney was signed to replace Al Del Greco, who retired as the franchise's top-ranked kicker following the 2000 season.

General manager Floyd Reese traded his first-round pick in the draft to the Saint Louis Rams in exchange for veteran Kevin Carter. The defensive end started opposite Jevon Kearse but failed to meet expectations, totaling just two sacks in his first season with the club.

Fifth-year receiver Derrick Mason signed a contract extension before the 2001 campaign after breaking the NFL record for all-purpose yards in a season (2,690) in 2000. He took advantage of an expanded role by posting the first 1,000-yard receiving season of his career, leading the team in yards (1,128), receptions (73), and touchdowns (9).

Eddie George missed the physical presence of blocking fullback Lorenzo Neal, who joined the Cincinnati Bengals in free agency. George averaged a career-low 3.0 yards per carry and failed to surpass the 1,000-yard mark for the first time since entering the league in 1996. He rushed for 939 yards and five touchdowns.

The defense faltered without Williams. The second-ranked scoring defense from 2000 dropped to 25th in Schwartz's first year as defensive coordinator, allowing 24.3 points per game.

After the season, the league announced that the Titans would move into the newly created AFC South Division in 2002.

Pro Bowl Selections

- Jevon Kearse (DE)
- Bruce Matthews (C)

Schedule

	OPPONENT	SCORE	RECORD
L	Miami Dolphins	23–31	0–1
L	@ Jacksonville Jaguars	6–13	0–2
L	@ Baltimore Ravens	7–26	0–3
W	Tampa Bay Buccaneers (OT)	31–28	1–3
W	@ Detroit Lions	27–24	2–3
L	@ Pittsburgh Steelers	7–34	2–4
W	Jacksonville Jaguars	28–24	3–4
L	Baltimore Ravens	10–16	3–5
W	@ Cincinnati Bengals	20–7	4–5
L	Pittsburgh Steelers	24–34	4–6
W	@ Cleveland Browns	31–15	5–6
L	@ Minnesota Vikings	24–42	5–7
W	Green Bay Packers	26–20	6–7
W	@ Oakland Raiders	13–10	7–7
L	Cleveland Browns	38–41	7–8
L	Cincinnati Bengals	21–23	7–9

Season Leaders

CATEGORY	TOTAL	PLAYER
Passing Yards	3,350	Steve McNair
Rushing Yards	939	Eddie George
Receiving Yards	1,128	Derrick Mason
Receptions	73	Derrick Mason
Interceptions	3	A. Dyson, S. Rolle
Sacks	10	Jevon Kearse
Points	94	Joe Nedney

Key Additions:
Drew Bennett (WR), Kevin Carter (DE)

Starting Lineup

OFFENSE	POSITION
Steve McNair	QB
Eddie George	RB
Kevin Dyson	WR
Derrick Mason	WR
Erron Kinney	TE
Frank Wycheck	TE
Brad Hopkins	LT
Zach Piller	LG
Bruce Matthews	C
Benji Olson	RG
Fred Miller	RT

DEFENSE	POSITION
Kevin Carter	DE
Josh Evans	DT
Jason Fisk	DT
Jevon Kearse	DE
Greg Favors	OLB
Randall Godfrey	MLB
Eddie Robinson	OLB
Andre Dyson	CB
Samari Rolle	CB
Aric Morris	SS
Perry Phenix	FS

SPECIAL TEAMS	POSITION
Joe Nedney	K
Derrick Mason	KR
Craig Hentrich	P
Derrick Mason	PR

Jevon Kearse was named to three Pro Bowls in three seasons before injuries slowed his career.

11–5

First in AFC South

Legendary offensive lineman Bruce Matthews retired at the conclusion of the 2001 season. The Titans inducted him into their Hall of Fame, retiring his number 74 jersey.

Tennessee drafted defensive tackle Albert Haynesworth with the 15th pick in the 2002 NFL Draft. Still within their championship window, the Titans aimed to bounce back from 2001's disappointment. However, they dropped four of their first five games. Then the Titans got hot, winning 10 of their final 11 contests. They dominated the new AFC South, compiling a perfect 6–0 record on their way to the divisional crown. They became the second Oilers/Titans team to qualify for the postseason after starting 1–4.

Eddie George became the franchise's all-time leading rusher in a thrilling overtime victory versus the New York Giants.

After a first-round bye in the playoffs, the second-seeded Titans hosted the Pittsburgh Steelers in the divisional round. The Titans jumped out to a commanding 14–0 advantage before the Steelers scored 20 consecutive points. After kicker Joe Nedney missed a 48-yard field goal to win the game, the back-and-forth affair sat at 31–31 at the end of regulation.

In overtime, Nedney missed again—this time from 31 yards. However, Steelers defensive back Dewayne Washington was controversially penalized for running into the kicker. Nedney converted the follow-up attempt, sending the Titans to their second AFC Championship Game in four years.

Against the Oakland Raiders, a pair of second-quarter fumbles by the Titans led to 10 points for Oakland, giving them momentum and a 24–17 lead. In the second half, the Raiders outscored the Titans, 17–7, and won a trip to Super Bowl XXXVII by a score of 41–24.

The defense took a significant step forward in Jim Schwartz's second season as the coordinator, even though defensive end Jevon Kearse missed 12 games due to injury.

Pro Bowl Selections

- Kevin Carter (DE)

Schedule

	OPPONENT	SCORE	RECORD
W	Philadelphia Eagles	27–24	1–0
L	@ Dallas Cowboys	13–21	1–1
L	Cleveland Browns (OT)	28–31	1–2
L	@ Oakland Raiders	25–52	1–3
L	Washington	14–31	1–4
W	Jacksonville Jaguars	23–14	2–4
W	@ Cincinnati Bengals	30–24	3–4
W	@ Indianapolis Colts	23–15	4–4
W	Houston Texans	17–10	5–4
W	Pittsburgh Steelers	31–23	6–4
L	@ Baltimore Ravens	12–13	6–5
W	@ New York Giants (OT)	32–29	7–5
W	Indianapolis Colts	27–17	8–5
W	New England Patriots	24–7	9–5
W	@ Jacksonville Jaguars	28–10	10–5
W	@ Houston Texans	13–3	11–5
W	*Pittsburgh Steelers (OT)*	*34–31*	*1–0*
L	*@ Oakland Raiders*	*24–41*	*1–1*

Season Leaders

CATEGORY	TOTAL	PLAYER
Passing Yards	3,387	Steve McNair
Rushing Yards	1,165	Eddie George
Receiving Yards	1,012	Derrick Mason
Receptions	79	Derrick Mason
Interceptions	6	Lance Schulters
Sacks	10	Kevin Carter
Points	111	Joe Nedney

Key Additions:
Albert Haynesworth (DT), Lance Schulters (S), Tank Williams (S)

Starting Lineup

OFFENSE	POSITION
Steve McNair	QB
Eddie George	RB
Kevin Dyson	WR
Derrick Mason	WR
Erron Kinney	TE
Frank Wycheck	TE
Brad Hopkins	LT
Zach Piller	LG
Gennaro DiNapoli	C
Benji Olson	RG
Fred Miller	RT

DEFENSE	POSITION
Kevin Carter	DE
John Thornton	DT
Henry Ford	DT
Carlos Hall	DE
Peter Sirmon	OLB
Randall Godfrey	MLB
Keith Bulluck	OLB
Andre Dyson	CB
Samari Rolle	CB
Tank Williams	SS
Lance Schulters	FS

SPECIAL TEAMS	POSITION
Joe Nedney	K
John Simon	KR
Craig Hentrich	P
John Simon	PR

Craig Hentrich spent 12 seasons with the Titans and was named to two Pro Bowls.

12–4

Second in AFC South

Head coach Jeff Fisher signed a multi-year extension ahead of the 2003 season. The Titans lost five players to free agency but didn't sign any free agents, partially due to difficulties against the salary cap.

In a rematch of the previous AFC Championship Game, the Titans opened the season against the Oakland Raiders on Sunday Night Football. The Titans got the better of the Raiders this time, winning 25–20 after punter Craig Hentrich drilled three field goals, following a season-ending injury to kicker Joe Nedney.

Steve McNair, who had gained a reputation for playing through pain, was injured in a Week 12 contest against the Atlanta Falcons. The Titans trailed, 21–0, in the first quarter. Backup quarterback Billy Volek replaced McNair with the Titans trailing, 21–14. Volek threw for 117 yards and a touchdown, helping to lead one of the largest come-from-behind wins in franchise history, 38–31.

Injuries to McNair and Volek forced third-string quarterback Neil O'Donnell to start Tennessee's regular-season finale. It would be the quarterback's final NFL appearance, a 33–13 win over the Tampa Bay Buccaneers. Eddie George became just the 17th running back in NFL history to surpass 10,000 rushing yards.

Despite a 12–4 record, the Titans had to settle for a wild-card spot in the playoffs. Against the Baltimore Ravens, the Titans got a game-winning, 46-yard field goal from Gary Anderson for a 20–17 victory.

Tennessee advanced to the divisional round to face Tom Brady and the New England Patriots in near-zero temperatures. Tennessee fell short in a defensive struggle, losing to the eventual Super Bowl champions, 17–14.

McNair was named the league's co-MVP, alongside Indianapolis's Peyton Manning. McNair, who became the second player in franchise history to win MVP, threw for a career-high 24 touchdowns and a career-low seven interceptions (minimum 10 appearances). His go-to target, Derrick Mason, posted a personal-best 1,303 receiving yards.

Schedule

	OPPONENT	SCORE	RECORD
W	Oakland Raiders	25–20	1–0
L	@ Indianapolis Colts	7–33	1–1
W	New Orleans Saints	27–12	2–1
W	@ Pittsburgh Steelers	30–13	3–1
L	@ New England Patriots	30–38	3–2
W	Houston Texans	38–17	4–2
W	@ Carolina Panthers	37–17	5–2
W	@ Jacksonville Jaguars	30–17	6–2
W	Miami Dolphins	31–7	7–2
W	Jacksonville Jaguars	10–3	8–2
W	@ Atlanta Falcons	38–31	9–2
L	@ New York Jets	17–24	9–3
L	Indianapolis Colts	27–29	9–4
W	Buffalo Bills	28–26	10–4
W	@ Houston Texans	27–24	11–4
W	Tampa Bay Buccaneers	33–13	12–4
W	*@ Baltimore Ravens*	*20–17*	*1–0*
L	*@ New England Patriots*	*14–17*	*1–1*

Season Leaders

CATEGORY	TOTAL	PLAYER
Passing Yards	3,215	Steve McNair
Rushing Yards	1,031	Eddie George
Receiving Yards	1,303	Derrick Mason
Receptions	95	Derrick Mason
Interceptions	6	Samari Rolle
Sacks	9.5	Jevon Kearse
Points	123	Gary Anderson

Key Additions:
Chris Brown (RB), Lamont Thompson (S)

Starting Lineup

Titans Trivia

Oilers legend Elvin Bethea (DE) was inducted into the Pro Football Hall of Fame in 2003.

Pro Bowl Selections

- Keith Bulluck (LB)
- Craig Hentrich (P)
- Brad Hopkins (OT)
- Derrick Mason (WR)
- Steve McNair (QB)

TITANS
85

Playoff Rivals

The Tennessee Titans and Baltimore Ravens have played some memorable postseason games over the years. The Ravens became a common opponent of the Titans in 1996 since the Baltimore-based franchise remained in the AFC Central Division after their relocation from Cleveland. The rivalry really began in the early 2000s when the franchises repeatedly crossed paths in the postseason.

The Titans entered the 2000 playoffs as the top seed in the AFC. Despite significantly outgaining the Ravens on offense, the Titans lost, 24–10. The Ravens blocked a field goal attempt in the fourth quarter and returned it for a 90-yard touchdown to take a 17–10 lead. A pick-six by linebacker Ray Lewis sealed the victory for Baltimore.

The two sides met again in the 2003 wild-card round. The Titans exacted revenge when veteran kicker Gary Anderson made a game-winning kick from 46 yards out, giving Tennessee a 20–17 victory.

The 13–3 Titans clinched the AFC's top seed in 2008. But game-changing running back Chris Johnson exited the contest in the second quarter with an ankle injury, leaving the Titans without their most dangerous playmaker. With the scored tied at 10, the Ravens hit a game-winning field goal to knock the Titans out of the playoffs.

In 2019, the Ravens were considered Super Bowl favorites after going 14–2 in the regular season. Powered by Derrick Henry's 195 rushing yards, the underdog Titans dominated the Ravens, winning 28–12.

Baltimore didn't wait long to retaliate. A year later, they defeated the Titans in the wild-card round, 20–13.

The next chapter awaits . . . .

In 2003, the Titans won, even though Derrick Mason was held to 28 yards receiving.

2004

5–11
Fourth in AFC South

Tight end Frank Wycheck announced his retirement after the 2003 season. Perhaps the greatest tight end in franchise history, he ranks third in team receptions (482), seventh in receiving yards (4,958), and 10th in touchdowns (27). The Titans released running back Eddie George. He left Tennessee as the franchise's all-time rushing leader with 10,009 yards. George would play the final season of his career with the Dallas Cowboys.

For the second consecutive offseason, the Titans weren't active in free agency. Instead, another major blow was dealt when Jevon Kearse signed with the Philadelphia Eagles. Recognizing that a lengthy rebuild had begun, general manager Floyd Reese traded his first-round draft pick to the Houston Texans in exchange for multiple picks. Veteran wide receiver Justin McCareins was also traded to the New York Jets for a second-round pick. The result of Reese's wheeling-and-dealing was a league-high 13 players drafted.

Injuries began taking a toll on quarterback Steve McNair, limiting him to eight games. Reserve quarterback Billy Volek started the other eight games and led the Titans in passing yards (2,486) and touchdowns (18).

A midseason game against the Chicago Bears ended in historic fashion. Volek fumbled in the end zone, and the resulting safety made Tennessee the second team ever to lose in overtime on a safety.

Both Drew Bennett and Derrick Mason surpassed 1,000 receiving yards, becoming the fifth duo in franchise history to achieve such a feat. It hadn't happened since 1991, when Haywood Jeffires and Drew Hill did the same.

Jim Schwartz's defensive unit allowed 27.4 points per game, which ranked 30 out of 32 teams. The Titans limped to a disappointing 5–11 record. It represented the franchise's worst season since 1994.

Schedule

	OPPONENT	SCORE	RECORD
W	@ Miami Dolphins	17–7	1–0
L	Indianapolis Colts	17–31	1–1
L	Jacksonville Jaguars	12–15	1–2
L	@ San Diego Chargers	17–38	1–3
W	@ Green Bay Packers	48–27	2–3
L	Houston Texans	10–20	2–4
L	@ Minnesota Vikings	3–20	2–5
W	Cincinnati Bengals	27–20	3–5
L	Chicago Bears (OT)	17–19	3–6
W	@ Jacksonville Jaguars	18–15	4–6
L	@ Houston Texans	21–31	4–7
L	@ Indianapolis Colts	24–51	4–8
L	Kansas City Chiefs	38–49	4–9
L	@ Oakland Raiders	35–40	4–10
L	Denver Broncos	16–37	4–11
W	Detroit Lions	24–19	5–11

Season Leaders

CATEGORY	TOTAL	PLAYER
Passing Yards	2,486	Billy Volek
Rushing Yards	1,067	Chris Brown
Receiving Yards	1,247	Drew Bennett
Receptions	96	Derrick Mason
Interceptions	6	Andre Dyson
Sacks	6	Kevin Carter
Points	88	Gary Anderson

Pro Bowl Selections

- None

Key Additions:
None

Brad Hopkins spent 13 seasons as the team's starting left tackle.

Starting Lineup

OFFENSE	POSITION
Billy Volek	QB
Chris Brown	RB
Robert Holcombe	RB
Drew Bennett	WR
Derrick Mason	WR
Erron Kinney	TE
Brad Hopkins	LT
Jacob Bell	LG
Justin Hartwig	C
Benji Olson	RG
Fred Miller	RT

DEFENSE	POSITION
Antwan Odom	DE
Kevin Carter	DT
Albert Haynesworth	DT
Carlos Hall	DE
Rocky Boiman	OLB
Brad Kassell	MLB
Keith Bulluck	OLB
Andre Dyson	CB
Samari Rolle	CB
Tank Williams	SS
Lamont Thompson	FS

SPECIAL TEAMS	POSITION
Gary Anderson	K
Jason McAddley	KR
Craig Hentrich	P
Derrick Mason	PR

2005

4–12
Third in AFC South

Head coach Jeff Fisher named Norm Chow his new offensive coordinator, replacing Mike Heimerdinger. It represented the 59-year-old's first opportunity in the NFL.

Ongoing difficulties against the salary cap forced the Titans to part with key players like Kevin Carter, Derrick Mason, Fred Miller, and Samari Rolle. Mason was released, despite enjoying his fourth consecutive 1,000-yard season in 2004. He and Rolle both signed with the rival Baltimore Ravens.

The Titans finally dipped back into the free-agent market by taking a flier on defensive end Kyle Vanden Bosch, a former second-round pick who failed to meet expectations with the Arizona Cardinals. He broke out of his shell in Tennessee, leading the team with 12.5 sacks.

With the sixth pick in the 2005 NFL Draft, general manager Floyd Reese selected cornerback Adam "Pacman" Jones. About two weeks prior to training camp, Jones was arrested for his alleged involvement in an incident at a night club. It would be the first of many run-ins with the law throughout Jones' tumultuous tenure as a Titan. The team also drafted a pair of offensive tackles in Michael Roos and David Stewart. In July, the Titans acquired veteran running back Travis Henry from the Buffalo Bills in exchange for a 2006 third-round pick.

Quarterback Steve McNair continued to battle through injuries, although he managed to appear in 14 games. The offense was further slowed by key departures and managed just a 21st-ranked 18.7 points per game. An inexperienced defense allowed a 29th-ranked 26.3 points per contest.

One of the most surprising bright spots was kicker Rob Bironas, who had previously bounced around different football leagues. He made nearly 80% of his field goals and scored 99 points.

Pro Bowl Selections

- Steve McNair (QB)
- Kyle Vanden Bosch (DE)

Schedule

	OPPONENT	SCORE	RECORD
L	@ Pittsburgh Steelers	7–34	0–1
W	Baltimore Ravens	25–10	1–1
L	@ Saint Louis Rams	27–31	1–2
L	Indianapolis Colts	10–31	1–3
W	@ Houston Texans	34–20	2–3
L	Cincinnati Bengals	23–31	2–4
L	@ Arizona Cardinals	10–20	2–5
L	Oakland Raiders	25–34	2–6
L	@ Cleveland Browns	14–20	2–7
L	Jacksonville Jaguars	28–31	2–8
W	San Francisco 49ers	33–22	3–8
L	@ Indianapolis Colts	3–35	3–9
W	Houston Texans	13–10	4–9
L	Seattle Seahawks	24–28	4–10
L	@ Miami Dolphins	10–24	4–11
L	@ Jacksonville Jaguars	13–40	4–12

Season Leaders

CATEGORY	TOTAL	PLAYER
Passing Yards	3,161	Steve McNair
Rushing Yards	851	Chris Brown
Receiving Yards	738	Drew Bennett
Receptions	58	Drew Bennett
Interceptions	3	Reynaldo Hill
Sacks	12.5	Kyle Vanden Bosch
Points	99	Rob Bironas

Key Additions:
Rob Bironas (K), Michael Roos (OT), David Stewart (OT), Kyle Vanden Bosch (DE)

In 11 seasons, Steve McNair posted a record of 76–55.

Starting Lineup

OFFENSE	POSITION
Steve McNair	QB
Chris Brown	RB
Drew Bennett	WR
Brandon Jones	WR
Ben Troupe	TE
Erron Kinney	TE
Brad Hopkins	LT
Zach Piller	LG
Justin Hartwig	C
Benji Olson	RG
Michael Roos	RT

DEFENSE	POSITION
Kyle Vanden Bosch	DE
Randy Starks	DT
Albert Haynesworth	DT
Antwan Odom	DE
Peter Sirmon	OLB
Brad Kassell	MLB
Keith Bulluck	OLB
Reynaldo Hill	CB
Adam Jones	CB
Tank Williams	SS
Lamont Thompson	FS

SPECIAL TEAMS	POSITION
Rob Bironas	K
Adam Jones	KR
Craig Hentrich	P
Adam Jones	PR

2006

8–8
Second in AFC South

The Titans were ready to move in a new direction at quarterback following consecutive injury-shortened campaigns for Steve McNair. In a controversial decision, they barred him from reporting to team headquarters in April. The team feared that another injury to McNair would lock them into paying what they deemed to be a bloated salary. A grievance was filed on McNair's behalf, and an arbitrator ruled in McNair's favor. Tennessee ultimately traded McNair to the Baltimore Ravens in June. How they handled McNair's highly publicized exit was a sore spot for fans.

Heading into the 2006 NFL Draft with the third overall pick, questions loomed about which quarterback the Titans would take. Rumors ran rampant that the organization was torn between quarterback prospects Jay Cutler, Matt Leinart, and Vince Young. (Years later, Jeff Fisher admitted that he wanted Cutler.) The Titans ultimately drafted Young, a dynamic dual-threat quarterback.

Days after McNair's trade, offensive tackle Brad Hopkins announced his retirement. He remains one of the greatest offensive linemen in Oilers/Titans history.

After the team was held to 10 points or fewer in two of their first three games, Young was named the starter—much earlier than anyone anticipated. He and the Titans got off to a bumpy start but hit their stride toward the end of the season. Young led the Titans to an unforgettable win over the New York Giants. Trailing 21–0, he spearheaded an offense that scored 24 unanswered points for a come-from-behind victory.

Two weeks later, the Titans defeated the Houston Texans in dramatic fashion. Young scrambled for a 39-yard game-winning touchdown in overtime, a play that became one of the most famous of his career.

The Titans entered Week 17 with an 8–7 record and with a chance to qualify for the postseason. Unfortunately, they were defeated, 40–23, by Tom Brady and the New England Patriots. Nevertheless, it was a successful season that had fans excited about the future. Young was awarded the NFL Offensive Rookie of the Year and was named to the Pro Bowl.

Schedule

	OPPONENT	SCORE	RECORD
L	New York Jets	16–23	0–1
L	@ San Diego Chargers	7–40	0–2
L	@ Miami Dolphins	10–13	0–3
L	Dallas Cowboys	14–45	0–4
L	@ Indianapolis Colts	13–14	0–5
W	@ Washington	25–22	1–5
W	Houston Texans	28–22	2–5
L	@ Jacksonville Jaguars	7–37	2–6
L	Baltimore Ravens	26–27	2–7
W	@ Philadelphia Eagles	31–13	3–7
W	New York Giants	24–21	4–7
W	Indianapolis Colts	20–17	5–7
W	@ Houston Texans (OT)	26–20	6–7
W	Jacksonville Jaguars	24–17	7–7
W	@ Buffalo Bills	30–29	8–7
L	New England Patriots	23–40	8–8

Season Leaders

CATEGORY	TOTAL	PLAYER
Passing Yards	2,199	Vince Young
Rushing Yards	1,211	Travis Henry
Receiving Yards	737	Drew Bennett
Receptions	46	Drew Bennett
Interceptions	5	Chris Hope
Sacks	6.5	Kyle Vanden Bosch
Points	98	Rob Bironas

Key Additions:
Cortland Finnegan (CB), Chris Hope (S), Kevin Mawae (C), Vince Young (QB)

Starting Lineup

Drew Bennett WR
Michael Roos LT
Jacob Bell LG
Kevin Mawae C
Benji Olson RG
David Stewart RT
Bo Scaife TE
Brandon Jones WR

Travis Henry RB
Vince Young QB
Ahmard Hall RB

CB Adam Jones
DE Travis LaBoy
DT Albert Haynesworth
DT Robaire Smith
DE Kyle Vanden Bosch
CB Reynaldo Hill

LB Keith Bulluck
LB Peter Sirmon
LB David Thornton

SS Chris Hope
FS Lamont Thompson

K Rob Bironas
KR Bobby Wade
P Craig Hentrich
PR Adam Jones

Titans Trivia

Warren Moon was inducted into the Pro Football Hall of Fame in 2006, and his jersey was retired by the franchise.

Pro Bowl Selections

- Vince Young (QB)

2007

10–6
Third in AFC South

General manager Floyd Reese stepped down after the 2006 season. Reese had held the position since 1994. The Titans hired former Oilers safety Mike Reinfeldt as Reese's replacement. Reinfeldt had most recently spent seven seasons in a front-office role with the Seattle Seahawks.

Cornerback Adam Jones was suspended for the entire season. He had five documented run-ins with police between February 2006 to February 2007. The most serious incident was Jones' alleged involvement in an altercation inside a gentleman's club in Las Vegas, where multiple patrons were injured following an alleged shooting. A member of Jones' entourage was the alleged shooter, and Jones would face multiple charges as a result.

Even without Jones, the Titans were spearheaded by the eighth-ranked scoring defense, which allowed just 18.6 points per game. In a dominant Monday Night Football victory over the New Orleans Saints, star linebacker Keith Bulluck intercepted three passes, earning him the nickname "Mr. Monday Night."

In Week 7, kicker Rob Bironas set an NFL record by making eight field goals against the Houston Texans.

The Titans ended the season on a three-game winning streak and clinched a playoff spot. In the wild-card round, Tennessee had a 6–0 advantage over the San Diego Chargers at halftime. However, the Chargers outscored the Titans 17–0 in the second half. Tennessee's struggling offense was held to 248 total yards in the game.

Legendary offensive lineman Bruce Matthews was inducted into the Pro Football Hall of Fame in 2007. Matthews became the first hall-of-famer to have worn a Titans uniform.

Pro Bowl Selections

- Rob Bironas (K)
- Albert Haynesworth (DT)
- Kyle Vanden Bosch (DE)

Schedule

	OPPONENT	SCORE	RECORD
W	@ Jacksonville Jaguars	13–10	1–0
L	Indianapolis Colts	20–22	1–1
W	@ New Orleans Saints	31–14	2–1
W	Atlanta Falcons	20–13	3–1
L	@ Tampa Bay Buccaneers	10–13	3–2
W	@ Houston Texans	38–36	4–2
W	Oakland Raiders	13–9	5–2
W	Carolina Panthers	20–7	6–2
L	Jacksonville Jaguars	13–28	6–3
L	@ Denver Broncos	20–34	6–4
L	@ Cincinnati Bengals	6–35	6–5
W	Houston Texans	28–20	7–5
L	San Diego Chargers (OT)	17–23	7–6
W	@ Kansas City Chiefs	26–17	8–6
W	New York Jets	10–6	9–6
W	@ Indianapolis Colts	16–10	10–6
L	*@ San Diego Chargers*	*6–17*	*0–1*

Season Leaders

CATEGORY	TOTAL	PLAYER
Passing Yards	2,546	Vince Young
Rushing Yards	1,110	LenDale White
Receiving Yards	750	Justin Gage
Receptions	55	J. Gage, R. Williams
Interceptions	5	Keith Bulluck
Sacks	12	Kyle Vanden Bosch
Points	133	Rob Bironas

Key Additions:
Michael Griffin (S)

Kyle Vanden Bosch was named to three Pro Bowls in five years.

Starting Lineup

OFFENSE	POSITION
Vince Young	QB
LenDale White	RB
Justin Gage	WR
Roydell Williams	WR
Ben Hartsock	TE
Bo Scaife	TE
Michael Roos	LT
Jacob Bell	LG
Kevin Mawae	C
Benji Olson	RG
David Stewart	RT

DEFENSE	POSITION
Antwan Odom	DE
Tony Brown	DT
Albert Haynesworth	DT
Kyle Vanden Bosch	DE
David Thornton	OLB
Ryan Fowler	MLB
Keith Bulluck	OLB
Nick Harper	CB
Cortland Finnegan	CB
Chris Hope	SS
Michael Griffin	FS

SPECIAL TEAMS	POSITION
Rob Bironas	K
Michael Griffin	KR
Craig Hentrich	P
Chris Davis	PR

2008

13–3
First in AFC South

Head coach Jeff Fisher replaced offensive coordinator Norm Chow by reuniting with Mike Heimerdinger. General manager Mike Reinfeldt selected running back Chris Johnson with the 24th pick in the draft. Johnson accounted for 1,488 total yards and 10 touchdowns as a rookie. His backup LenDale White rushed for 15 touchdowns as a goal-line specialist.

Quarterback Vince Young entered the season on thin ice. In the opening game, he was booed after throwing a late interception. A few plays later, he suffered a sprained knee and was replaced by Kerry Collins. Later that month, concerns about Young's mental health and well-being led Fisher to announce that Young would serve as Collins' backup when healthy.

Collins and the Titans improved to a franchise-best 10–0 start before losing to the New York Jets. A few weeks later, a showdown with the Pittsburgh Steelers loomed large. The Titans stood at 12–2, while the Steelers were 11–3. Tennessee proved to be legitimate Super Bowl contenders by dominating the Steelers, 31–14, clinching the AFC's top seed and home-field advantage throughout the playoffs. Several Titans players stomped on the Steelers' "Terrible Towel" in the dying seconds. Steelers fans were enraged.

After a first-round bye, the Titans hosted the Baltimore Ravens. Midway through the second quarter, Johnson exited the game with an ankle injury. At the time of his departure, Johnson had already rushed for 72 yards and a touchdown. (Years later, he would claim that the Ravens had attempted to deliberately injure him.) Without their best playmaker and plagued by untimely turnovers, the Titans never got going. With help from a controversial delay-of-game penalty that went uncalled, the Ravens won on a late field goal, 13–10.

Pro Bowl Selections

- Kerry Collins (QB)
- Cortland Finnegan (CB)
- Michael Griffin (S)
- Albert Haynesworth (DT)
- Chris Hope (S)
- Chris Johnson (RB)
- Kevin Mawae (C)
- Michael Roos (OT)

Schedule

	OPPONENT	SCORE	RECORD
W	Jacksonville Jaguars	17–10	1–0
W	@ Cincinnati Bengals	24–7	2–0
W	Houston Texans	31–12	3–0
W	Minnesota Vikings	30–17	4–0
W	@ Baltimore Ravens	13–10	5–0
W	@ Kansas City Chiefs	34–10	6–0
W	Indianapolis Colts	31–21	7–0
W	Green Bay Packers (OT)	19–16	8–0
W	@ Chicago Bears	21–14	9–0
W	@ Jacksonville Jaguars	24–14	10–0
L	New York Jets	13–34	10–1
W	@ Detroit Lions	47–10	11–1
W	Cleveland Browns	28–9	12–1
L	@ Houston Texans	12–13	12–2
W	Pittsburgh Steelers	31–14	13–2
L	@ Indianapolis Colts	0–23	13–3
L	*Baltimore Ravens*	*10–13*	*0–1*

Season Leaders

CATEGORY	TOTAL	PLAYER
Passing Yards	2,676	Kerry Collins
Rushing Yards	1,228	Chris Johnson
Receiving Yards	651	Justin Gage
Receptions	58	Bo Scaife
Interceptions	7	Michael Griffin
Sacks	8.5	Albert Haynesworth
Points	127	Rob Bironas

Key Additions:
Chris Johnson (RB)

Starting Lineup

OFFENSE	POSITION
Kerry Collins	QB
Chris Johnson	RB
Ahmard Hall	RB
Justin Gage	WR
Justin McCareins	WR
Alge Crumpler	TE
Michael Roos	LT
Eugene Amano	LG
Kevin Mawae	C
Jake Scott	RG
David Stewart	RT

DEFENSE	POSITION
Jevon Kearse	DE
Tony Brown	DT
Albert Haynesworth	DT
Kyle Vanden Bosch	DE
David Thornton	OLB
Stephen Tulloch	MLB
Keith Bulluck	OLB
Nick Harper	CB
Cortland Finnegan	CB
Chris Hope	SS
Michael Griffin	FS

SPECIAL TEAMS	POSITION
Rob Bironas	K
Chris Carr	KR
Craig Hentrich	P
Chris Carr	PR

Albert Haynesworth was a First-Team All-Pro defensive tackle in both 2007 and 2008.

2009

8–8
Third in AFC South

Defensive coordinator Jim Schwartz left the team to become the Detroit Lions' head coach. Secondary coach Chuck Cecil was promoted to replace him.

Ahead of the 2009 campaign, the Titans couldn't afford to re-sign defensive tackle Albert Haynesworth. The star free agent inked a historic deal with Washington worth $100 million. (It ultimately proved to be one of the worst high-cost signings in the history of free agency.)

Tragedy struck the organization on July 4, when 36-year-old Steve McNair was shot and killed. The Titans honored the franchise legend by holding a two-day memorial at LP Field. The team wore a commemorative "9" sticker on their helmets throughout the season, in memory of him.

In Week 6, the Titans were defeated, 59–0, by the New England Patriots. It represented the worst loss in franchise history and brought the Titans' record to 0–6, a shockingly poor start for a franchise that had won 13 games the season prior. After the loss, Tennessee moved on from veteran quarterback Kerry Collins in favor of Vince Young.

Young led the Titans to a dominant victory over the Jacksonville Jaguars, completing 83.3% of his passing attempts. Running back Chris Johnson continued his unstoppable streak (see page 134) with a franchise-record 228 rushing yards in the win over Jacksonville.

That began a five-game winning streak, which included a come-from-behind victory over the Arizona Cardinals. Trailing 17–13, Young led a 99-yard game-winning drive that culminated in a 10-yard touchdown pass to rookie receiver Kenny Britt as time expired. Young miraculously converted three fourth-down attempts on the drive.

Once again, Young looked like a potential franchise quarterback.

Pro Bowl Selections

- Chris Johnson (RB)
- Kevin Mawae (C)
- Kyle Vanden Bosch (DE)
- Vince Young (QB)

Schedule

	OPPONENT	SCORE	RECORD
L	@ Pittsburgh Steelers (OT)	10–13	0–1
L	Houston Texans	31–34	0–2
L	@ New York Jets	17–24	0–3
L	@ Jacksonville Jaguars	17–37	0–4
L	Indianapolis Colts	9–31	0–5
L	@ New England Patriots	0–59	0–6
W	Jacksonville Jaguars	30–13	1–6
W	@ San Francisco 49ers	34–27	2–6
W	Buffalo Bills	41–17	3–6
W	@ Houston Texans	20–17	4–6
W	Arizona Cardinals	20–17	5–6
L	@ Indianapolis Colts	17–27	5–7
W	Saint Louis Rams	47–7	6–7
W	Miami Dolphins (OT)	27–24	7–7
L	San Diego Chargers	17–42	7–8
W	@ Seattle Seahawks	17–13	8–8

Season Leaders

CATEGORY	TOTAL	PLAYER
Passing Yards	1,879	Vince Young
Rushing Yards	2,006	Chris Johnson
Receiving Yards	701	Kenny Britt
Receptions	50	Chris Johnson
Interceptions	5	Cortland Finnegan
Sacks	5.5	Jacob Ford
Points	118	Rob Bironas

Key Additions:
Kenny Britt (WR), Jared Cook (TE), Jason McCourty (CB), Brett Kern (P), Nate Washington (WR)

Starting Lineup

OFFENSE	POSITION
Vince Young	QB
Chris Johnson	RB
Ahmard Hall	RB
Justin Gage	WR
Nate Washington	WR
Alge Crumpler	TE
Michael Roos	LT
Eugene Amano	LG
Kevin Mawae	C
Jake Scott	RG
David Stewart	RT

DEFENSE	POSITION
William Hayes	DE
Jovan Haye	DT
Tony Brown	DT
Kyle Vanden Bosch	DE
David Thornton	OLB
Stephen Tulloch	MLB
Keith Bulluck	OLB
Nick Harper	CB
Cortland Finnegan	CB
Chris Hope	SS
Michael Griffin	FS

SPECIAL TEAMS	POSITION
Rob Bironas	K
Kenny Britt	KR
Brett Kern	P
Alvin Pearman	PR

Players and fans shared a moment of silence for Steve McNair before the first preseason game.

The Run for 2,000

The 2009 campaign is best remembered for the breathtaking individual performances put forth by superstar running back Chris Johnson. In Week 2, he rushed for 197 yards and two touchdowns in a 34–31 loss to the Houston Texans. Johnson's elite, game-changing speed was on display with scores of 91 and 57 yards—not to mention a 69-yard touchdown reception.

The Titans entered the Week 7 bye at a hapless 0–6, but Johnson began salvaging the season in Week 8. He rushed for a franchise-record 228 yards and two touchdowns in a dominant 30–13 victory over the Jacksonville Jaguars. It was Johnson's second in a historic 11-game in-season streak of 100-plus rushing yards.

In Week 12, Johnson ran for an 85-yard touchdown in a thrilling come-from-behind triumph over the Arizona Cardinals.

In the regular-season finale versus the Seattle Seahawks, Johnson rushed for 134 yards and two touchdowns, crossing the 2,000-yard mark. He finished the season with 2,006 rushing yards, becoming just the sixth running back to surpass 2,000 yards on the ground in a single season (joining O.J. Simpson, Eric Dickerson, Barry Sanders, Terrell Davis, and Jamal Lewis).

The dual-threat Johnson, who also led the Titans in receptions, set an NFL record for the most scrimmage yards in a single season with 2,509, surpassing the mark previously set by Marshall Faulk in 1999. Johnson was named the NFL Offensive Player of the Year.

TITANS
28

All-2000s Offense

QUARTERBACK: Steve McNair (1995–2005) qualified for three Pro Bowls and was named NFL co-MVP in 2003. McNair ranks second in franchise history in passing yards (27,141) and third in touchdown passes (156). His 76 regular-season wins rank first in franchise history among quarterbacks. McNair gained entrance into the Oilers/Titans newly formed Ring of Honor in 2008. His jersey was retired by the club in 2019.

RUNNING BACKS: Eddie George (1996–2003) never missed a start with the franchise, playing in 128 straight games. In 2000, he rushed for a career-best 1,509 yards and 14 touchdowns. George remains the franchise's all-time leader in rushing yards (10,009). He also entered the Oilers/Titans new Ring of Honor in 2008, and his jersey was retired in 2019. Chris Johnson (2008–2013) accounted for 1,488 total yards as a rookie. He had a historic season in 2009, rushing for 2,006 yards and earning NFL Offensive Player of the Year. Johnson set the NFL's single-season record for yards from scrimmage that season with 2,509.

WIDE RECEIVERS: In 2001, Derrick Mason (1997–2004) posted his first of four consecutive 1,000-yard receiving seasons for the Titans. He ranks fifth all-time in receptions for the franchise (453), sixth in receiving yards (6,114), and sixth in receiving touchdowns (37). Drew Bennett (2001–2006) led the Titans in receiving yards in 2004, 2005, and 2006. Bennett posted a career-best 1,247 yards and 11 touchdowns in 2004.

TIGHT END: Even toward the back end of his career, Frank Wycheck (1995–2003) was the Titans' most impressive tight end of the decade. He recorded back-to-back 600-yard seasons in 2000 and 2001, accounting for eight touchdowns across that period. He was inducted into the Oilers/Titans new Ring of Honor in 2008.

CENTER: Kevin Mawae (2006–2009) was already a six-time Pro Bowler when he joined the Titans. He quickly became a team captain and was voted to two more Pro Bowls during his four seasons in Nashville. Mawae was voted into the Pro Football Hall of Fame in 2019.

GUARDS: Zach Piller (1999–2006) started 58 career games for the Titans. He helped them qualify for back-to-back playoff appearances in 2002 and 2003. Benji Olson (1998–2007) was a steady performer throughout the decade, starting 123 of a possible 128 regular-season games.

TACKLES: In 2008, Michael Roos (2005–2014) was named a First-Team All-Pro. He was a key member of a dominant offensive line that tied for allowing a league-low 12 sacks. Brad Hopkins (1993–2005) was a 13-year starter for the team. He was named to the Pro Bowl in 2000 and 2003.

KICKER: In 2007, Rob Bironas (2005–2013) made a career-high 35 field goals and scored 133 points. Bironas was First-Team All-Pro for his efforts. He remained effective throughout the second half of the decade and beyond.

KICK RETURNER: Derrick Mason (1997–2004) was a dynamic kick returner in 2000. He averaged 27.0 yards per return, which ranked second in the league. Mason was also the primary kick returner in 2001, averaging an effective 22.0 yards per return.

Statistics for the all-decade team are for the given decade only, unless otherwise noted.

All-2000s Defense

DEFENSIVE ENDS: At the end of the 1990s, Jevon Kearse (1999–2003, 2008–2009) enjoyed arguably the best rookie season in Titans history. During the 2000s, he was slowed by injury but recorded 37.5 sacks and was named to two Pro Bowls. Kyle Vanden Bosch (2005–2009) was one of the greatest free-agent signings in Titans history. In his first season with the club, he had 12.5 sacks. Vanden Bosch was named to three Pro Bowls in five seasons with the Titans.

DEFENSIVE TACKLES: One of the greatest interior defensive linemen in Titans history, Albert Haynesworth (2002–2008) was particularly dominant throughout the two-year stretch of 2007 and 2008, totaling 14.5 sacks. Haynesworth was named to the Pro Bowl and was First-Team All-Pro both seasons. Kevin Carter (2001–2004) was primarily a defensive end, but he selflessly agreed to switch positions in 2004. He made a flawless transition, leading the Titans in sacks with six. Carter was named to the Pro Bowl as a defensive end in 2002.

LINEBACKERS: One of the great defenders in Titans history, Keith Bulluck (2000–2009) recorded 100+ tackles in five straight seasons. Bulluck recorded 19 interceptions and forced 15 fumbles throughout his 10-year run as a Titan. Randall Godfrey (2000–2002) posted a career-high 121 tackles in 2000, forced five fumbles, and added three sacks. He was twice named AFC Defensive Player of the Week and earned Second-Team All-Pro honors. David Thornton (2006–2010) racked up 369 tackles between 2006 and 2009, including consecutive 100-tackle seasons in 2006 and 2007.

CORNERBACKS: Samari Rolle (1998–2004) led the team in interceptions with a career-high of seven in 2000. Rolle was named First-Team All-Pro as a result. He led the Titans in interceptions on two more occasions and totaled 19 interceptions this decade. Some around the league considered Cortland Finnegan (2006–2011) "dirty," but Titans fans called him "scrappy." He scored pick-six touchdowns in three straight seasons in 2008, 2009, and 2010, including a historic 99-yarder against the Houston Texans in 2008.

SAFETIES: A leader on the field, Chris Hope (2006–2011) recorded 16 interceptions with the Titans. He earned Pro Bowl honors in 2008. Michael Griffin (2007–2015) earned back-to-back Pro Bowl nods in 2008 and 2009. A tackling machine, he surpassed 100 tackles in three seasons.

PUNTER: Craig Hentrich (1998–2009) was especially outstanding in 2003, when he was named to the Pro Bowl. Hentrich ranks second all-time in Oilers/Titans punting yards (36,926).

PUNT RETURNER: Derrick Mason (1997–2004) led the league in yards gained via punt returns in 2000 with 662. That ranks as the highest single-season total in Oilers/Titans history.

Keith Bulluck led the NFL in 2004 with 152 total tackles.

2010

6–10
Fourth in AFC South

The Titans lost several veterans in free agency. Kyle Vanden Bosch signed with the Detroit Lions, and the Titans did not pursue a contract extension with linebacker Keith Bulluck, who had suffered a serious knee injury in 2009. They also let center Kevin Mawae go, and he ultimately retired. Running back LenDale White was traded to the Seattle Seahawks on draft weekend.

In Week 4, Tennessee's first-round draft pick, Derrick Morgan, suffered a season-ending knee injury. A week later, the Titans claimed an exciting victory over the Dallas Cowboys. Vince Young threw two touchdowns, and Chris Johnson scampered for 131 yards and two touchdowns, including a game-winning score in the fourth quarter as the Titans prevailed, 34–27.

Kerry Collins started for an injured Young against the Philadelphia Eagles. Wide receiver Kenny Britt amassed career highs in receiving yards (225) and touchdowns (three), leading the Titans to victory, 37–19. The 5–2 Titans were averaging an explosive 28.4 points per game. That's when things fell apart. Tennessee dropped their next six games.

Fans were excited when the Titans claimed legendary receiver Randy Moss off waivers, but the results were disappointing. Moss recorded just six receptions for 80 receiving yards in eight games.

In Week 11, Young suffered a thumb injury, and the Titans lost in overtime. Young stripped off his uniform and tossed his shoulder pads into the stands of a disappointed home crowd. After a heated exchange with head coach Jeff Fisher, Young was placed on season-ending injured reserve and was asked to stay home.

Rookie quarterback Rusty Smith started one game before Collins started Tennessee's final five contests. The disappointing 2010 season represented the end of a long-lasting era. (See page 140.)

Schedule

	OPPONENT	SCORE	RECORD
W	Oakland Raiders	38–13	1–0
L	Pittsburgh Steelers	11–19	1–1
W	@ New York Giants	29–10	2–1
L	Denver Broncos	20–26	2–2
W	@ Dallas Cowboys	34–27	3–2
W	@ Jacksonville Jaguars	30–3	4–2
W	Philadelphia Eagles	37–19	5–2
L	@ San Diego Chargers	25–33	5–3
L	@ Miami Dolphins	17–29	5–4
L	Washington (OT)	16–19	5–5
L	@ Houston Texans	0–20	5–6
L	Jacksonville Jaguars	6–17	5–7
L	Indianapolis Colts	28–30	5–8
W	Houston Texans	31–17	6–8
L	@ Kansas City Chiefs	14–34	6–9
L	@ Indianapolis Colts	20–23	6–10

Season Leaders

CATEGORY	TOTAL	PLAYER
Passing Yards	1,823	Kerry Collins
Rushing Yards	1,364	Chris Johnson
Receiving Yards	775	Kenny Britt
Receptions	44	Chris Johnson
Interceptions	4	Michael Griffin
Sacks	12.5	Jason Babin
Points	110	Rob Bironas

Pro Bowl Selections

- Jason Babin (DE)
- Michael Griffin (S)
- Chris Johnson (RB)
- Marc Mariani (KR/PR)

Key Additions:
Jason Babin (DE), Derrick Morgan (DE), Alterraun Verner (CB)

Starting Lineup

OFFENSE	POSITION
Vince Young	QB
Chris Johnson	RB
Nate Washington	WR
Kenny Britt	WR
Bo Scaife	TE
Craig Stevens	TE
Michael Roos	LT
Leroy Harris	LG
Eugene Amano	C
Jake Scott	RG
David Stewart	RT

DEFENSE	POSITION
Jason Babin	DE
Jason Jones	DT
Tony Brown	DT
Dave Ball	DE
Gerald McRath	OLB
Stephen Tulloch	MLB
Will Witherspoon	OLB
Alterraun Verner	CB
Cortland Finnegan	CB
Chris Hope	SS
Michael Griffin	FS

SPECIAL TEAMS	POSITION
Rob Bironas	K
Marc Mariani	KR
Brett Kern	P
Marc Mariani	PR

"Discipline is doing what you don't want to do, so you can do what you really want to do."
—Jeff Fisher

In 2010, Michael Griffin was Second-Team All-Pro.

9–7

Second in AFC South

Jeff Fisher and the Titans agreed to part ways following the turbulent 2010 season. Fisher left as the winningest coach in Titans history, compiling 147 victories (including the playoffs). The Titans named offensive line coach Mike Munchak, who had been on staff since 1995, as Fisher's replacement. Munchak hired Jerry Gray as defensive coordinator and Chris Palmer as offensive coordinator. Legendary ex-player Bruce Matthews was hired as the offensive line coach.

Owner Bud Adams announced that quarterback Vince Young wouldn't return. His career with the Titans could be summarized by "what if." Young often electrified fans but was inconsistent and endured several off-field setbacks that stalled his progress.

Entering the 2011 NFL Draft in search of a new quarterback, the Titans drafted Jake Locker with the eighth overall pick. Understanding that Locker was a developmental talent, the Titans signed veteran quarterback Matt Hasselbeck in free agency to be the starter. Mike Reinfeldt made one of his best decisions as Titans general manager in the third round, drafting defensive tackle Jurrell Casey.

Running back Chris Johnson and the Titans were involved in a lengthy contract-related standoff. They reached a six-year, $56 million agreement just before the start of the season. Johnson rushed for 1,047 yards and four touchdowns, averaging a career-low 4.0 yards per carry.

Hasselbeck delivered one of the best single-season passing performances in Titans history, throwing for 3,571 yards and 18 touchdowns. He was effective despite losing his top wide receiver, Kenny Britt, to a season-ending knee injury in Week 3. Nate Washington picked up the slack by recording a 1,000-yard season. Locker played sparingly, making just five appearances. The Titans outperformed expectations, finishing 9–7, but they fell short of making the playoffs.

Schedule

	OPPONENT	SCORE	RECORD
L	@ Jacksonville Jaguars	14–16	0–1
W	Baltimore Ravens	26–13	1–1
W	Denver Broncos	17–14	2–1
W	@ Cleveland Browns	31–13	3–1
L	@ Pittsburgh Steelers	17–38	3–2
L	Houston Texans	7–41	3–3
W	Indianapolis Colts	27–10	4–3
L	Cincinnati Bengals	17–24	4–4
W	@ Carolina Panthers	30–3	5–4
L	@ Atlanta Falcons	17–23	5–5
W	Tampa Bay Buccaneers	23–17	6–5
W	@ Buffalo Bills	23–17	7–5
L	New Orleans Saints	17–22	7–6
L	@ Indianapolis Colts	13–27	7–7
W	Jacksonville Jaguars	23–17	8–7
W	@ Houston Texans	23–22	9–7

Season Leaders

CATEGORY	TOTAL	PLAYER
Passing Yards	3,571	Matt Hasselbeck
Rushing Yards	1,047	Chris Johnson
Receiving Yards	1,023	Nate Washington
Receptions	74	Nate Washington
Interceptions	2	M. Griffin, J. McCourty
Sacks	7	Karl Klug
Points	121	Rob Bironas

Pro Bowl Selections

- None

Key Additions:
Jurrell Casey (DT)

Starting Lineup

OFFENSE	POSITION
Matt Hasselbeck	QB
Chris Johnson	RB
Ahmard Hall	RB
Nate Washington	WR
Damian Williams	WR
Craig Stevens	TE
Michael Roos	LT
Leroy Harris	LG
Eugene Amano	C
Jake Scott	RG
David Stewart	RT

DEFENSE	POSITION
Derrick Morgan	DE
Sen'Derrick Marks	DT
Jurrell Casey	DT
Jason Jones	DE
Akeem Ayers	OLB
Barrett Ruud	MLB
Will Witherspoon	OLB
Jason McCourty	CB
Cortland Finnegan	CB
Jordan Babineaux	SS
Michael Griffin	FS

SPECIAL TEAMS	POSITION
Rob Bironas	K
Marc Mariani	KR
Brett Kern	P
Marc Mariani	PR

Rob Bironas made more than 90% of his field goal attempts in 2010 and 2011.

6–10

Third in AFC South

General manager Mike Reinfeldt was promoted to senior executive vice president and chief operating officer (but would be let go less than a year later). Ruston Webster was promoted to general manager.

The Titans spent a portion of the offseason in a furious pursuit of free-agent and future hall-of-fame quarterback Peyton Manning. Owner Bud Adams publicly professed a desire to sign him. Manning was already a local legend, having played college football at the University of Tennessee. Titans fans obsessed over the potential of adding him to the team, and Tennessee remained one of Manning's final choices—but the four-time league MVP chose to join the Denver Broncos instead. The news was met with great disappointment from Titans fans.

Tennessee's all-in approach with Manning led to a lackluster free agency period. They lost defensive contributors such as Cortland Finnegan and Chris Hope. Webster added a pass rusher in Kamerion Wimbley and signed veteran guard Steve Hutchinson. Neither stood out in 2012. Webster drafted wide receiver Kendall Wright with the 20th selection in the 2012 NFL Draft. Wright led the team in receptions as a rookie with 64 and tied for the team lead in receiving touchdowns with four.

Despite receiving stellar play from Matt Hasselbeck in 2011, Jake Locker was named the starting quarterback. Locker led the Titans to an exciting come-from-behind overtime victory versus the Detroit Lions in Week 3. He threw for 378 yards in a historic performance that saw the team score five touchdowns of 60-plus yards. A week later, Locker suffered an injury that forced him to miss several games.

In late November, head coach Mike Munchak attempted to spark the offense by firing offensive coordinator Chris Palmer. Quarterbacks coach Dowell Loggains was promoted in his place. Weeks later, superstar running back Chris Johnson rushed for a franchise-long 94-yard touchdown. It was a highlight of a forgettable 6–10 season.

Locker's inconsistent and injury-riddled campaign delivered more questions than answers about his long-term outlook.

Schedule

	OPPONENT	SCORE	RECORD
L	New England Patriots	13–34	0–1
L	@ San Diego Chargers	10–38	0–2
W	Detroit Lions (OT)	44–41	1–2
L	@ Houston Texans	14–38	1–3
L	@ Minnesota Vikings	7–30	1–4
W	Pittsburgh Steelers	26–23	2–4
W	@ Buffalo Bills	35–34	3–4
L	Indianapolis Colts (OT)	13–19	3–5
L	Chicago Bears	20–51	3–6
W	@ Miami Dolphins	37–3	4–6
L	@ Jacksonville Jaguars	19–24	4–7
L	Houston Texans	10–24	4–8
L	@ Indianapolis Colts	23–27	4–9
W	New York Jets	14–10	5–9
L	@ Green Bay Packers	7–55	5–10
W	Jacksonville Jaguars	38–20	6–10

Season Leaders

CATEGORY	TOTAL	PLAYER
Passing Yards	2,176	Jake Locker
Rushing Yards	1,243	Chris Johnson
Receiving Yards	746	Nate Washington
Receptions	64	Kendall Wright
Interceptions	4	M. Griffin, J. McCourty
Sacks	6.5	Derrick Morgan
Points	110	Rob Bironas

Key Additions:
Kendall Wright (WR)

Starting Lineup

Titans Trivia

In Week 17, the Titans became the first team to score two punt return touchdowns and two pick-sixes in the same game.

Chris Johnson's 94-Yard Run

2012

Pro Bowl Selections

- None

2013

7–9

Second in AFC South

General manager Ruston Webster was aggressive in free agency. He signed guard Andy Levitre to a six-year, $46.8 million contract. The Titans also signed tight end Delanie Walker to a four-year deal. Walker surpassed expectations with his offensive contributions. Other additions included veteran quarterback Ryan Fitzpatrick, who replaced Matt Hasselbeck, as well as defensive starters Moise Fokou, Sammie Lee Hill, and Bernard Pollard.

Webster selected guard Chance Warmack with the 10th pick in the 2013 NFL Draft. Warmack was viewed by many as a can't-miss prospect, but he struggled as a rookie. Starting quarterback Jake Locker continued to be injury-prone. He saw action in just seven games but posted a record of 4–3. Fitzpatrick started the team's final seven games.

On October 21, 2013, founding owner K.S. "Bud" Adams, Jr., passed away at the age of 90. Adams was a trailblazer whose vision helped shape professional football. Adams' son-in-law Tommy Smith was named team president and CEO following Adams' passing. Adams' daughters, Susie Adams Smith and Amy Adams Hunt, were named co-chairpersons. Adams' grandson, Kenneth Adams IV, became a member of the board of directors.

The organization mourned the loss of Adams during their bye week, and they honored his memory when they returned to the field on November 3 by defeating Jeff Fisher's Saint Louis Rams, 28–21. Chris Johnson ran for 150 yards and scored the game-winning touchdown in the fourth quarter.

Johnson recorded his sixth consecutive 1,000-yard season but averaged a career-low as a Titan of 3.9 yards per carry. It would be his last season in Tennessee. Wide receiver Kendall Wright had a breakout season with 94 receptions for 1,079 yards. Third-year defensive tackle Jurrell Casey became a defensive superstar. He tallied 10.5 sacks.

Despite improvement from young players, it felt to many like another wasted season. Many of Webster's big additions failed to make an impact. The Titans improved just marginally, finishing 7–9. That wasn't good enough for Tennessee's new leadership, who made sweeping changes in the offseason.

Schedule

	OPPONENT	SCORE	RECORD
W	@ Pittsburgh Steelers	16–9	1–0
L	@ Houston Texans (OT)	24–30	1–1
W	San Diego Chargers	20–17	2–1
W	New York Jets	38–13	3–1
L	Kansas City Chiefs	17–26	3–2
L	@ Seattle Seahawks	13–20	3–3
L	San Francisco 49ers	17–31	3–4
W	@ Saint Louis Rams	28–21	4–4
L	Jacksonville Jaguars	27–29	4–5
L	Indianapolis Colts	27–30	4–6
W	@ Oakland Raiders	23–19	5–6
L	@ Indianapolis Colts	14–22	5–7
L	@ Denver Broncos	28–51	5–8
L	Arizona Cardinals (OT)	34–37	5–9
W	@ Jacksonville Jaguars	20–16	6–9
W	Houston Texans	16–10	7–9

Season Leaders

CATEGORY	TOTAL	PLAYER
Passing Yards	2,454	Ryan Fitzpatrick
Rushing Yards	1,077	Chris Johnson
Receiving Yards	1,079	Kendall Wright
Receptions	94	Kendall Wright
Interceptions	5	Alterraun Verner
Sacks	10.5	Jurrell Casey
Points	116	Rob Bironas

Key Additions:
Delanie Walker (TE)

Starting Lineup

Titans Trivia

In 2008, Bud Adams received the Pro Football Hall of Fame's Lamar Hunt Award for his contributions to the sport and the league.

Bud Adams Passes Away

2013

Pro Bowl Selections

- Alterraun Verner (CB)

O. SMITH
45
27
34

Eddie! Eddie! Eddie!

General manager Floyd Reese selected running back Eddie George with the 14th overall pick in the 1996 NFL Draft—one year after selecting quarterback Steve McNair. The move gave the franchise two offensive superstars to build around.

As a rookie, George ran for 1,368 yards and eight touchdowns. His efforts were rewarded with NFL Offensive Rookie of the Year honors.

George built on that success as a sophomore by rushing for 1,399 yards and six touchdowns on the way to his first Pro Bowl nod. George was a consistent threat across 1998 and 1999, gaining 2,598 rushing yards and scoring 14 touchdowns over those two seasons. He helped the Titans advance to Super Bowl XXXIV in 1999.

George's best season came in 2000. He rushed for career highs in yards (1,509) and touchdowns (14), earning a trip to his fourth (and final) Pro Bowl. Injuries and heavy workloads began catching up to George, and he was eventually released from his contract following the 2003 season.

George sits atop the franchise's all-time leader board in rushing yards with 10,009. He remains the only Oilers/Titans running back to surpass 10,000 rushing yards. He is certainly on the franchise's Mount Rushmore as an all-time great.

George received a place in the Oilers/Titans Ring of Honor in 2008. He was inducted into the College Football Hall of Fame in 2011. As of 2024, he has been a semifinalist for the Pro Football Hall of Fame.

In 2000, Eddie George led the NFL with 403 rushing attempts and 453 total touches. The totals are fifth most and third most in NFL history, respectively.

2014

2–14
Fourth in AFC South

The Titans parted ways with head coach Mike Munchak after he refused to fire his assistant coaches. Ken Whisenhunt was hired in his place. The former Arizona Cardinals head coach was in high demand, and the Titans aggressively pursued him. Whisenhunt assembled a veteran staff that included Ray Horton as defensive coordinator and Mike Mularkey as tight ends coach.

The Titans selected offensive tackle Taylor Lewan with the 11th pick in the draft. He was seen as the eventual successor to Michael Roos, who was nearing the end of his career.

Despite six consecutive 1,000-yard seasons, running back Chris Johnson was released from his contract. Cornerback Alterraun Verner joined the Tampa Bay Buccaneers in free agency, and former first-round receiver Kenny Britt signed with the Saint Louis Rams. Right tackle David Stewart was released, as was kicker Rob Bironas. Bironas's 239 field goals rank second in franchise history, and his 1,032 career points are just 28 points shy of all-time franchise leader Al Del Greco. During the 2014 season, Bironas was tragically killed in a single-vehicle accident on a night that allegedly included alcohol use and road-rage incidents.

Entering a fate-deciding season, quarterback Jake Locker continued to see his career derailed by injury. Locker spent most of the season playing sporadically, and it became clear that the Titans were going to move on from him in the offseason. Veteran journeyman Charlie Whitehurst and seventh-round rookie Zach Mettenberger combined to start 11 games, together going 1–10 and confirming that Tennessee would need to start over at quarterback.

Whisenhunt's Titans ended the 2014 campaign on a 10-game losing streak and finishing at 2–14, the team's worst record since 1994. The offense averaged a 30th-ranked 15.9 points per game, while the defense allowed a 29th-ranked 27.4 points per game. Tight end Delanie Walker was a lone bright spot. In just his second season as a Titan, he set the franchise's single-season record for receiving yards by a tight end with 890, breaking Frank Wycheck's previous mark of 768 set in 1998.

Schedule

	OPPONENT	SCORE	RECORD
W	@ Kansas City Chiefs	26–10	1–0
L	Dallas Cowboys	10–26	1–1
L	@ Cincinnati Bengals	7–33	1–2
L	@ Indianapolis Colts	17–41	1–3
L	Cleveland Browns	28–29	1–4
W	Jacksonville Jaguars	16–14	2–4
L	@ Washington	17–19	2–5
L	Houston Texans	16–30	2–6
L	@ Baltimore Ravens	7–21	2–7
L	Pittsburgh Steelers	24–27	2–8
L	@ Philadelphia Eagles	24–43	2–9
L	@ Houston Texans	21–45	2–10
L	New York Giants	7–36	2–11
L	New York Jets	11–16	2–12
L	@ Jacksonville Jaguars	13–21	2–13
L	Indianapolis Colts	10–27	2–14

Season Leaders

CATEGORY	TOTAL	PLAYER
Passing Yards	1,412	Zach Mettenberger
Rushing Yards	569	Bishop Sankey
Receiving Yards	890	Delanie Walker
Receptions	63	Delanie Walker
Interceptions	3	Jason McCourty
Sacks	6.5	Derrick Morgan
Points	84	Ryan Succop

Key Additions:
DaQuan Jones (DE), Taylor Lewan (OT), Wesley Woodyard (LB)

Starting Lineup

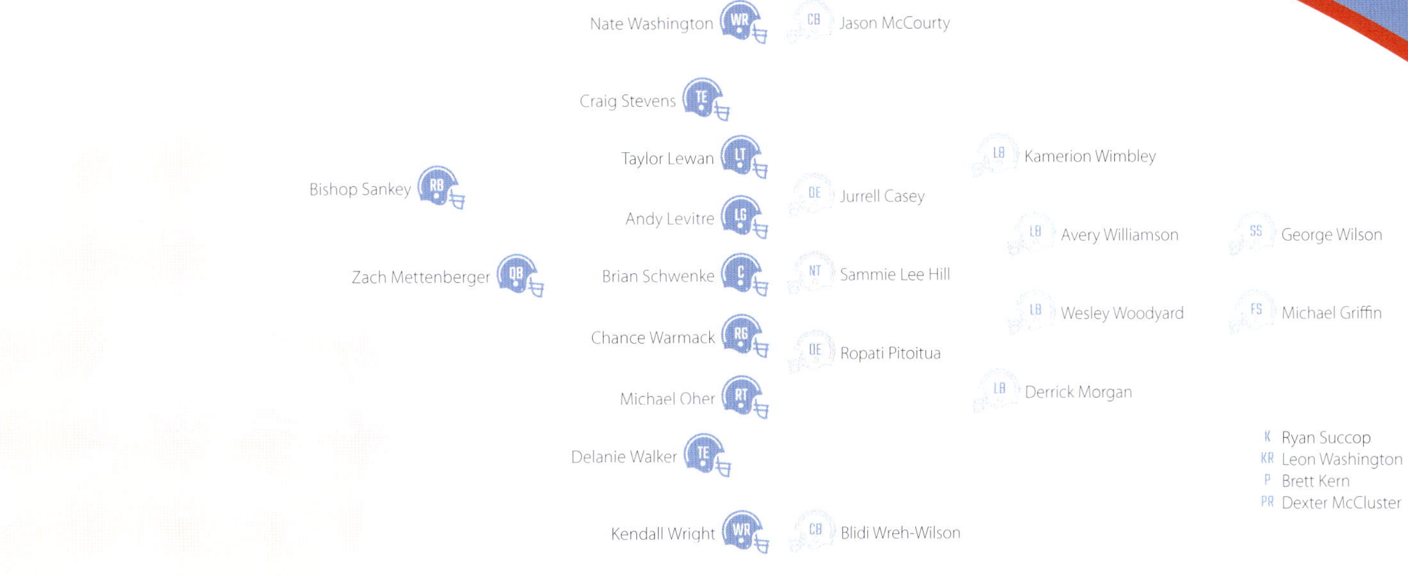

Titans Trivia

In 2014, Zach Mettenberger managed eight touchdown passes, tied for the team's lowest leading total in the Titans era of football.

Pro Bowl Selections

- None

3–13

Fourth in AFC South

After NFL commissioner Roger Goodell began seeking clarity on the Tennessee Titans' ownership structure, Amy Adams Strunk started representing the family in ownership-related manners as the team's controlling owner. LP Field was renamed Nissan Stadium, and head coach Ken Whisenhunt hired coaching legend Dick LeBeau as a defensive assistant. LeBeau worked directly with defensive coordinator Ray Horton to implement the defense.

Quarterback Jake Locker shockingly announced his retirement after just four seasons in the league. In desperate need of a signal-caller, general manager Ruston Webster selected Marcus Mariota with the second overall pick in the 2015 NFL Draft. Webster signed multiple players in free agency, including pass rusher Brian Orakpo. Before the season opener, the Titans traded left guard Andy Levitre to the Atlanta Falcons for draft capital.

Mariota's debut was legendary. He completed 13 of 15 pass attempts for 209 yards and four touchdowns in a 42–14 blowout of the Tampa Bay Buccaneers. He became the second rookie ever to throw four touchdown passes in his debut (Fran Tarkenton, 1961). Mariota earned a perfect passer rating of 158.3 and was later named the NFL Rookie of the Month for September.

That performance proved to be misleading. After a loss to the Houston Texans dropped the team to 1–6, Whisenhunt was fired. With a record of 3–20, his .130 win percentage ranks as second-worst in franchise history, trailing Bill Peterson (1–18, .053). Assistant head coach and tight ends coach Mike Mularkey was named interim head coach. The team responded to Mularkey by claiming a 34–28 overtime victory over the New Orleans Saints.

Delanie Walker became the first (and only) tight end in franchise history to surpass 1,000 receiving yards in a single season. He finished with 1,088.

Pro Bowl Selections

- Jurrell Casey (DT)
- Delanie Walker (TE)

Schedule

OPPONENT	SCORE	RECORD
@ Tampa Bay Buccaneers	42–14	1–0
@ Cleveland Browns	14–28	1–1
Indianapolis Colts	33–35	1–2
Buffalo Bills	13–14	1–3
Miami Dolphins	10–38	1–4
Atlanta Falcons	7–10	1–5
@ Houston Texans	6–20	1–6
@ New Orleans Saints (OT)	34–28	2–6
Carolina Panthers	10–27	2–7
@ Jacksonville Jaguars	13–19	2–8
Oakland Raiders	21–24	2–9
Jacksonville Jaguars	42–39	3–9
@ New York Jets	8–30	3–10
@ New England Patriots	16–33	3–11
Houston Texans	6–34	3–12
@ Indianapolis Colts	24–30	3–13

Season Leaders

CATEGORY	TOTAL	PLAYER
Passing Yards	2,818	Marcus Mariota
Rushing Yards	520	Antonio Andrews
Receiving Yards	1,088	Delanie Walker
Receptions	94	Delanie Walker
Interceptions	2	Z. Brown, C. Sensabaugh
Sacks	7	J. Casey, B. Orakpo
Points	71	Ryan Succop

Key Additions:
Marcus Mariota (QB), Brian Orakpo (LB)

Jurrell Casey was named to his first of five straight Pro Bowls in 2015.

Starting Lineup

OFFENSE	POSITION
Marcus Mariota	QB
Antonio Andrews	RB
Harry Douglas	WR
Kendall Wright	WR
Delanie Walker	TE
Anthony Fasano	TE
Taylor Lewan	LT
Quinton Spain	LG
Brian Schwenke	C
Chance Warmack	RG
Byron Bell	RT

DEFENSE	POSITION
DaQuan Jones	DE
Al Woods	NT
Jurrell Casey	DE
Derrick Morgan	OLB
Wesley Woodyard	ILB
Avery Williamson	ILB
Brian Orakpo	OLB
Perrish Cox	CB
Coty Sensabaugh	CB
Da'Norris Searcy	SS
Michael Griffin	FS

SPECIAL TEAMS	POSITION
Ryan Succop	K
Dexter McCluster	KR
Brett Kern	P
Dexter McCluster	PR

2016

9–7
Second in AFC South

General manager Ruston Webster was fired, and the Titans hired Jon Robinson in his place. Mike Mularkey became the official head coach. He hired Terry Robiskie as offensive coordinator and promoted Dick LeBeau to defensive coordinator.

Robinson's first major move as general manager was to acquire running back DeMarco Murray in a trade with the Philadelphia Eagles. Murray, a former NFL Offensive Player of the Year, proved to be a brilliant acquisition, totaling 1,664 yards and 12 touchdowns in 2016. Robinson continued putting his stamp on the team by trading wide receiver Dorial Green-Beckham to the Eagles for offensive tackle Dennis Kelly. Robinson also made outstanding additions in free agency, adding center Ben Jones and wide receiver Rishard Matthews.

Two weeks before the 2016 NFL Draft, Robinson traded the first overall pick to the Los Angeles Rams for a haul that included two first-round picks, two second-round picks, and two third-round picks. On draft day, Robinson traded back into the top 10 to select offensive tackle Jack Conklin. He used a second-round pick on running back Derrick Henry and a third-rounder on safety Kevin Byard.

The moves led to a significantly improved team. In Weeks 5–10, the Titans scored an average of 33.7 points per game.

A three-game winning streak had the Titans entering a Week 16 matchup with the Jacksonville Jaguars at 8–6 with an opportunity to strengthen their chances of making the postseason. Unfortunately, Mariota suffered a season-ending injury. The Titans were defeated and were eliminated from playoff contention. The season ended in disappointment, but the progress shown throughout 2016 signaled that the future was bright.

Schedule

	OPPONENT	SCORE	RECORD
L	Minnesota Vikings	16–25	0–1
W	@ Detroit Lions	16–15	1–1
L	Oakland Raiders	10–17	1–2
L	@ Houston Texans	20–27	1–3
W	@ Miami Dolphins	30–17	2–3
W	Cleveland Browns	28–26	3–3
L	Indianapolis Colts	26–34	3–4
W	Jacksonville Jaguars	36–22	4–4
L	@ San Diego Chargers	35–43	4–5
W	Green Bay Packers	47–25	5–5
L	@ Indianapolis Colts	17–24	5–6
W	@ Chicago Bears	27–21	6–6
W	Denver Broncos	13–10	7–6
W	@ Kansas City Chiefs	19–17	8–6
L	@ Jacksonville Jaguars	17–38	8–7
W	Houston Texans	24–17	9–7

Season Leaders

CATEGORY	TOTAL	PLAYER
Passing Yards	3,426	Marcus Mariota
Rushing Yards	1,287	DeMarco Murray
Receiving Yards	945	Rishard Matthews
Receptions	65	R. Matthews, D. Walker
Interceptions	3	Perrish Cox
Sacks	10.5	Brian Orakpo
Points	105	Ryan Succop

Pro Bowl Selections

- Jurrell Casey (DT)
- Taylor Lewan (OT)
- DeMarco Murray (RB)
- Brian Orakpo (LB)
- Delanie Walker (TE)

Key Additions:
Kevin Byard (S), Jack Conklin (OT), Ben Jones (C), Derrick Henry (RB), DeMarco Murray (RB)

Taylor Lewan started 100 games for the Titans in his nine-year career.

Starting Lineup

OFFENSE	POSITION
Marcus Mariota	QB
DeMarco Murray	RB
Rishard Matthews	WR
Tajaé Sharpe	WR
Anthony Fasano	TE
Delanie Walker	TE
Taylor Lewan	LT
Quinton Spain	LG
Ben Jones	C
Josh Kline	RG
Jack Conklin	RT

DEFENSE	POSITION
DaQuan Jones	DE
Al Woods	NT
Jurrell Casey	DE
Derrick Morgan	OLD
Wesley Woodyard	ILB
Avery Williamson	ILB
Brian Orakpo	OLB
Perrish Cox	CB
Jason McCourty	CB
Da'Norris Searcy	SS
Rashad Johnson	FS

SPECIAL TEAMS	POSITION
Ryan Succop	K
Marc Mariani	KR
Brett Kern	P
Marc Mariani	PR

9–7
Second in AFC South

The Titans had two first-round selections in 2017. With them, general manager Jon Robinson drafted wide receiver Corey Davis and cornerback Adoree' Jackson.

The season was a roller-coaster ride. After starting 2–3, the Titans won six of their next seven—including back-to-back divisional triumphs over the Indianapolis Colts and Houston Texans.

Three consecutive losses to NFC teams threatened to derail the season. The 8–7 Titans entered their regular-season finale versus the Jacksonville Jaguars with their playoff fate in their own hands. A win would send the Titans to the postseason. The game was a defensive struggle; the only offensive touchdown scored by either team was a 66-yard catch and run at the start of the second quarter by Derrick Henry. The young running back also had 28 rushing attempts but was held to 51 yards. Three field goals by Ryan Succop proved the difference for the Titans. A defensive touchdown by the Jaguars in the fourth quarter kept the game close, but Kevin Byard made a game-clinching interception. The Titans won, 15–10.

The Titans' wild-card opponent was the Kansas City Chiefs. The underdog Titans were down 21–3 at halftime. But quarterback Marcus Mariota led Tennessee to three second-half touchdowns, including one incredible play that saw Mariota catch his own touchdown pass. The Titans won a thriller, 22–21. It was Tennessee's first playoff victory in 14 years, and one of the greatest come-from-behind victories in Titans history. It also tied the second-biggest comeback ever in the postseason by a road team.

The Titans were defeated in the divisional round, 35–14, by Tom Brady and the New England Patriots. Even though the Titans took a step forward in 2017, owner Amy Adams Strunk decided it was time for change.

Schedule

OPPONENT	SCORE	RECORD
Oakland Raiders	16–26	0–1
@ Jacksonville Jaguars	37–16	1–1
Seattle Seahawks	33–27	2–1
@ Houston Texans	14–57	2–2
@ Miami Dolphins	10–16	2–3
Indianapolis Colts	36–22	3–3
@ Cleveland Browns (OT)	12–9	4–3
Baltimore Ravens	23–20	5–3
Cincinnati Bengals	24–20	6–3
@ Pittsburgh Steelers	17–40	6–4
@ Indianapolis Colts	20–16	7–4
Houston Texans	24–13	8–4
@ Arizona Cardinals	7–12	8–5
@ San Francisco 49ers	23–25	8–6
Los Angeles Rams	23–27	8–7
Jacksonville Jaguars	15–10	9–7
@ Kansas City Chiefs	*22–21*	*1–0*
@ New England Patriots	*14–35*	*1–1*

Season Leaders

CATEGORY	TOTAL	PLAYER
Passing Yards	3,232	Marcus Mariota
Rushing Yards	744	Derrick Henry
Receiving Yards	807	Delanie Walker
Receptions	74	Delanie Walker
Interceptions	8	Kevin Byard
Sacks	7.5	Derrick Morgan
Points	136	Ryan Succop

Pro Bowl Selections

- Kevin Byard (S)
- Jurrell Casey (DT)
- Brett Kern (P)
- Taylor Lewan (OT)
- Brynden Trawick (ST)
- Delanie Walker (TE)

Key Additions:
Corey Davis (WR), Logan Ryan (CB), Jonnu Smith (TE)

Starting Lineup

OFFENSE	POSITION
Marcus Mariota	QB
DeMarco Murray	RB
Rishard Matthews	WR
Corey Davis	WR
Jonnu Smith	TE
Delanie Walker	TE
Taylor Lewan	LT
Quinton Spain	LG
Ben Jones	C
Josh Kline	RG
Jack Conklin	RT

DEFENSE	POSITION
DaQuan Jones	DE
Sylvester Williams	DT
Jurrell Casey	DE
Derrick Morgan	OLB
Wesley Woodyard	ILB
Avery Williamson	ILB
Brian Orakpo	OLB
Adoree' Jackson	CB
Logan Ryan	CB
Johnathan Cyprien	SS
Kevin Byard	FS

SPECIAL TEAMS	POSITION
Ryan Succop	K
Adoree' Jackson	KR
Brett Kern	P
Adoree' Jackson	PR

"You just have to be your best and, no matter what, do what you can do and affect the things that you can control."
—Marcus Mariota

Kevin Byard tied for the NFL lead with eight interceptions in 2017.

2018

9–7
Third in AFC South

Controlling owner Amy Adams Strunk and general manager Jon Robinson decided to let head coach Mike Mularkey go. Mike Vrabel was hired as the new coach. Vrabel chose Matt LaFleur as his offensive coordinator and Dean Pees as his defensive coordinator.

The 2018 campaign began in peculiar fashion. The Week 1 contest with the Miami Dolphins lasted seven-plus hours due to multiple weather delays. The Titans were eventually defeated, 27–20, in the league's longest game since the 1970 AFL-NFL merger. Quarterback Marcus Mariota exited with an elbow injury that cost him the next two games. Star tight end Delanie Walker suffered a season-ending injury in the defeat.

In Week 7, the Titans lost, 20–19, to the Los Angeles Chargers at Wembley Stadium in London, England—the Titans' first regular-season contest to take place overseas.

Running back Derrick Henry gained a franchise-record 238 rushing yards in a 30–9 blowout victory over the Jacksonville Jaguars. He ran for a historic 99-yard touchdown, stiff-arming multiple Jaguars defenders en route to an NFL-record-tying run. Henry scored four touchdowns in the triumph, tying a franchise record. The season turned out to be Henry's breakout campaign as he rushed for 1,059 yards and 12 touchdowns, beginning a multi-year streak of dominance that would cement Henry's legacy as an all-time great.

The Titans entered their regular-season finale against the Indianapolis Colts at 9–6 and in control of their own destiny. A win would send them to the playoffs. However, Mariota was unable to play due to a nerve injury. Without him, the Titans were defeated, 33–17, by quarterback Andrew Luck and the Colts.

Serious doubts arose about Mariota's future with the team, following recurring injuries and inconsistent play. He was under contract for one more season, but Tennessee would acquire a high-upside backup quarterback in the offseason, giving them some much-needed depth in case Mariota's struggles continued.

Schedule

	OPPONENT	SCORE	RECORD
L	@ Miami Dolphins	20–27	0–1
W	Houston Texans	20–17	1–1
W	@ Jacksonville Jaguars	9–6	2–1
W	Philadelphia Eagles (OT)	26–23	3–1
L	@ Buffalo Bills	12–13	3–2
L	Baltimore Ravens	0–21	3–3
L	@ L.A. Chargers *(London)*	19–20	3–4
W	@ Dallas Cowboys	28–14	4–4
W	New England Patriots	34–10	5–4
L	@ Indianapolis Colts	10–38	5–5
L	@ Houston Texans	17–34	5–6
W	New York Jets	26–22	6–6
W	Jacksonville Jaguars	30–9	7–6
W	@ New York Giants	17–0	8–6
W	Washington	25–16	9–6
L	Indianapolis Colts	17–33	9–7

Season Leaders

CATEGORY	TOTAL	PLAYER
Passing Yards	2,528	Marcus Mariota
Rushing Yards	1,059	Derrick Henry
Receiving Yards	891	Corey Davis
Receptions	65	Corey Davis
Interceptions	4	Kevin Byard
Sacks	7	Jurrell Casey
Points	106	Ryan Succop

Key Additions:
Malcolm Butler (CB), Harold Landry (LB)

Starting Lineup

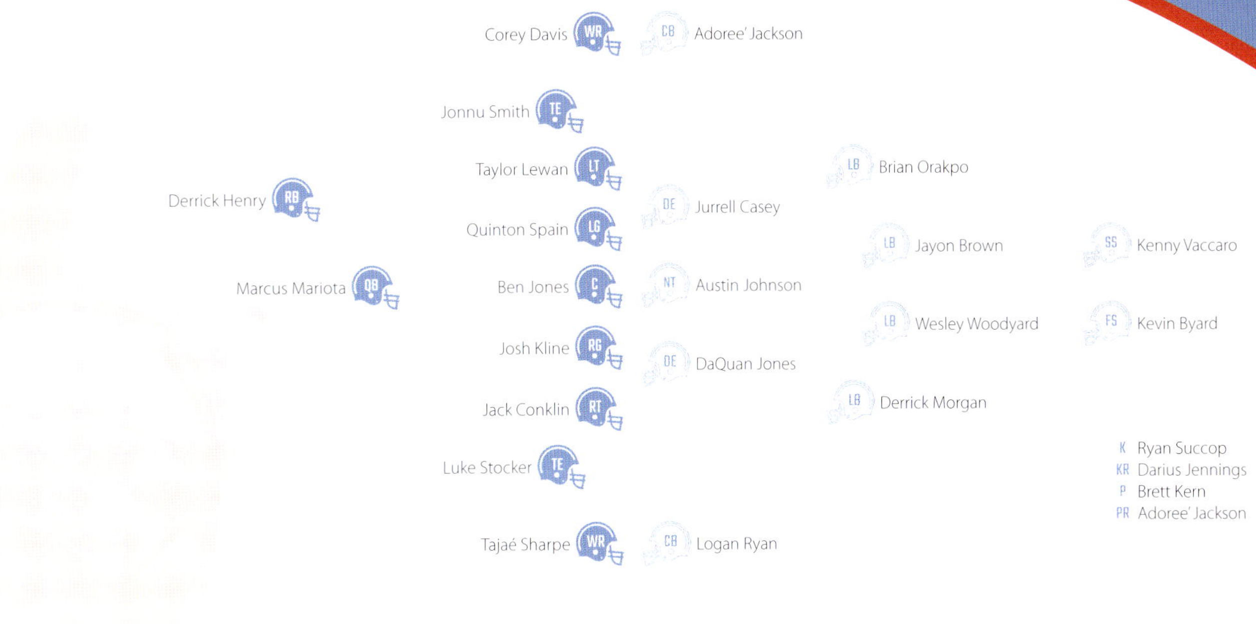

Titans Trivia

The Titans unveiled new uniforms in 2018, the first major change to the franchise's uniforms since becoming the Titans in 1999.

Pro Bowl Selections

- Jurrell Casey (DT)
- Brett Kern (P)
- Taylor Lewan (OT)

9–7

Second in AFC South

Titans offensive coordinator Matt LaFleur was hired as the Green Bay Packers head coach in the offseason. Mike Vrabel promoted tight ends coach Arthur Smith to replace him. General manager Jon Robinson acquired veteran quarterback Ryan Tannehill in a trade with the Miami Dolphins.

Nashville hosted the 2019 NFL Draft, and more than 600,000 fans attended the three-day spectacle—setting an NFL attendance record. The Titans drafted defensive tackle Jeffery Simmons in the first round and wide receiver A.J. Brown in the second. Overall, it ranked among the greatest drafts in Titans history, with the team landing five multi-year starters.

After an impressive Week 1 performance, the Titans offense struggled. In Week 6, Tennessee suffered an embarrassing 16–0 loss to the Denver Broncos. Mariota was benched midway through the game, and the team made the decision to start Tannehill moving forward. With Tannehill under center, the Titans compiled a record of 7–3. Tannehill won the NFL Comeback Player of the Year.

In the playoffs, the Titans defeated the New England Patriots, 20–13, in the wild-card round. Henry was a workhorse, gaining 204 total yards from scrimmage. Notably, it was quarterback Tom Brady's final game as a Patriot.

Tennessee's dreamlike season continued as they rolled into Baltimore and dominated the top-seeded Ravens, beating them, 28–12. Henry rushed for 195 yards and threw a three-yard touchdown pass. Henry became the first running back to gain more than 175 rushing yards twice in the same postseason.

The Titans fell short in the AFC Championship Game. Patrick Mahomes and the Kansas City Chiefs won, 35–24. Nevertheless, the 2019 campaign is remembered as one of the most exciting in franchise history.

Pro Bowl Selections

- Jurrell Casey (DT)
- Derrick Henry (RB)
- Brett Kern (P)
- Ryan Tannehill (QB)

Schedule

	OPPONENT	SCORE	RECORD
W	@ Cleveland Browns	43–13	1–0
L	Indianapolis Colts	17–19	1–1
L	@ Jacksonville Jaguars	7–20	1–2
W	@ Atlanta Falcons	24–10	2–2
L	Buffalo Bills	7–14	2–3
L	@ Denver Broncos	0–16	2–4
W	Los Angeles Chargers	23–20	3–4
W	Tampa Bay Buccaneers	27–23	4–4
L	@ Carolina Panthers	20–30	4–5
W	Kansas City Chiefs	35–32	5–5
W	Jacksonville Jaguars	42–20	6–5
W	@ Indianapolis Colts	31–17	7–5
W	@ Oakland Raiders	42–21	8–5
L	Houston Texans	21–24	8–6
L	New Orleans Saints	28–38	8–7
W	@ Houston Texans	35–14	9–7
W	*@ New England Patriots*	*20–13*	*1–0*
W	*@ Baltimore Ravens*	*28–12*	*2–0*
L	*@ Kansas City Chiefs*	*24–35*	*2–1*

Season Leaders

CATEGORY	TOTAL	PLAYER
Passing Yards	2,742	Ryan Tannehill
Rushing Yards	1,540	Derrick Henry
Receiving Yards	1,051	A.J. Brown
Receptions	52	A.J. Brown
Interceptions	5	Kevin Byard
Sacks	9	Harold Landry
Points	108	Derrick Henry

Key Additions:
A.J. Brown (WR), Rodger Saffold (G), Jeffery Simmons (DT), Ryan Tannehill (QB)

In 2019, Ryan Tannehill's passer rating of 117.5 was the best in the NFL.

Starting Lineup

OFFENSE	POSITION
Ryan Tannehill	QB
Derrick Henry	RB
Corey Davis	WR
A.J. Brown	WR
Jonnu Smith	TE
MyCole Pruitt	TE
Taylor Lewan	LT
Rodger Saffold	LG
Ben Jones	C
Nate Davis	RG
Jack Conklin	RT

DEFENSE	POSITION
Jeffery Simmons	DE
DaQuan Jones	NT
Jurrell Casey	DE
Kamalei Correa	OLB
Rashaan Evans	ILB
Jayon Brown	ILB
Harold Landry	OLB
Logan Ryan	CB
Adoree' Jackson	CB
Kenny Vaccaro	SS
Kevin Byard	FS

SPECIAL TEAMS	POSITION
Ryan Succop	K
Kalif Raymond	KR
Brett Kern	P
Adam Humphries	PR

All-2010s Offense

QUARTERBACK: Perhaps a controversial decision, Ryan Tannehill (2019–2023) gets the start on the All-Decade team, despite playing for just one season in the decade. He was that good in his one season, and the rest of the quarterback play throughout the decade was sporadic.

RUNNING BACKS: Derrick Henry (2016–2023) started slowly as DeMarco Murray's backup, but he led the team in rushing in his second year. In 2019, he led the NFL in rushing yards with 1,540 and in rushing touchdowns with 16. From 2010 to 2013, Chris Johnson (2008–2013) compiled four consecutive 1,000-yard rushing seasons. A dual-threat as a receiver, he gained nearly 6,000 yards from scrimmage across those four seasons.

WIDE RECEIVERS: Nate Washington (2009–2014) was a model of consistency. His best showing as a Titan came in 2011 when he led the team in receptions (74) and receiving yards (1,023). Through 2023, Washington ranks eighth all-time in franchise history for receiving yards (4,591) and 10th in receptions (307). Although it was tempting to include A.J. Brown here, Kendall Wright (2012–2016) contributed for five seasons. He led the Titans in receptions (64) as a rookie, and he had a team-high 94 catches for 1,079 yards in his second season.

TIGHT END: Delanie Walker (2013–2019) is one of the greatest free-agent signings in Titans history. In 2014, he became the Titans' single-season receiving yards leader among all tight ends (890). He followed that by breaking his own record, becoming the only tight end in franchise history to record 1,000 receiving yards in a season.

CENTER: A model of toughness, reliability, and grit, Ben Jones (2016–2022) developed into the anchor of some excellent offensive lines. Jones was a two-time team captain who missed just one of 97 games throughout his first six seasons with the team.

GUARDS: Quinton Spain (2015–2018) enjoyed three quality seasons as a starter. He helped DeMarco Murray lead the AFC in rushing yards and helped pave the way for Henry's first 1,000-yard season. Rodger Safford and Jake Scott also garnered consideration, but Josh Kline (2016–2018) played well over three seasons, starting in 46 games and earning a place on our All-Decade team.

TACKLES: Taylor Lewan (2014–2022) made the All-Rookie Team and later was named to three consecutive Pro Bowls. Lewan was a big reason behind Henry's rushing success. Jack Conklin (2016–2019) made the All-Rookie Team and was a steady performer throughout his time with the Titans.

KICKER: Ryan Succop (2014–2019) scored 136 points in 2017, which is tied with Al Del Greco (1998) for the single-season franchise record. Succop's 117 career field goals is tied for third most in Oilers/Titans history.

KICK RETURNER: Marc Mariani (2010–2013, 2016) was named to the Pro Bowl as a rookie after scoring two touchdowns as a special teams returner (one kickoff return, one punt return). His 1,530 kickoff return yards in 2010 rank as the franchise's all-time single-season best.

Statistics for the all-decade team are for the given decade only, unless otherwise noted.

All-2010s Defense

DEFENSIVE ENDS: Jurrell Casey (2011–2019) is among the greatest Titans defenders of all time. In 2013, he recorded a team-best and career-high 10.5 sacks. Casey was voted to five consecutive Pro Bowls, and he led the Titans in sacks again in 2015 and 2018. DaQuan Jones (2014–2020) played multiple positions across the defensive line. Better known for his run-stopping ability, Jones did the dirty work that didn't always receive box-score recognition. He appeared in 99 games for the Titans in seven seasons.

NOSE TACKLE: Al Woods (2014–2016) appeared in 42 games for the Titans across three seasons. He totaled 66 tackles, including nine for a loss. In 2016, he anchored a defensive line that allowed a second-best 88.3 rushing yards per game.

LINEBACKERS: Derrick Morgan (2010–2018) was an underrated performer. He made a successful transition from defensive end to outside linebacker to fit a change in defensive scheme. Morgan totaled 44.5 sacks in nine seasons. Brian Orakpo (2015–2018) tallied 24.5 sacks throughout his first three seasons in Tennessee. He was a Pro Bowl player in 2016 after enjoying a 10.5-sack season. Wesley Woodyard (2014–2019) and Avery Williamson (2014–2017) were starters at inside linebacker together from 2014 to 2017. Williamson totaled 376 tackles with the Titans, leading the team twice. Woodyard accumulated 517 tackles, including a team-high 124 in 2017.

CORNERBACKS: Jason McCourty (2009–2016) appeared in 108 games with 90 starts for the franchise. He led the team in interceptions three times. Logan Ryan (2017–2019) added experience and a winning pedigree. He was especially outstanding in 2019, when he totaled 113 tackles, broke up a career-high 18 passes, had four interceptions, and forced a personal-best four fumbles.

SAFETIES: Kevin Byard (2016–2023) shined as a full-time starter in his second year, recording a career-high eight interceptions. Byard is tied for fourth all-time on the franchise's interceptions leader board with 27. Michael Griffin (2007–2015) was a mainstay in the lineup between 2010 and 2015, starting 92 games. He recorded 108 tackles and four interceptions in 2010 en route to Pro Bowl and Second-Team All-Pro honors.

PUNTER: Brett Kern (2009–2021) is the greatest punter in Titans history. He was named to three Pro Bowls this decade and was First-Team All-Pro in 2019. He ranks as the team's career leader in gross punting average (45.9) and net punting average (40.8) among players with 150 or more punts.

PUNT RETURNER: Marc Mariani (2010–2013, 2016) scored touchdowns as a punt returner in back-to-back seasons in 2010 and 2011. Mariani came back as the punt returner in 2016.

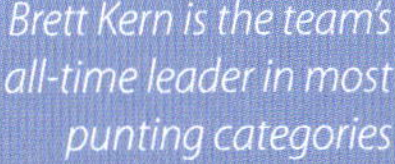

Brett Kern is the team's all-time leader in most punting categories

2020

11–5
First in AFC South

The Titans parted ways with two decorated players ahead of the 2020 campaign. Defensive tackle Jurrell Casey was traded to the Denver Broncos, and tight end Delanie Walker was released. Both are counted among the Titan greats. The team doubled down on their 2019 success by signing quarterback Ryan Tannehill and running back Derrick Henry to long-term extensions.

The COVID-19 pandemic drastically impacted the league. In-person events were modified, the preseason was canceled, and the 2020 NFL Draft was held virtually. The Titans drafted offensive tackle Isaiah Wilson with their first-round pick, which proved to be among the worst selections in franchise history. Wilson was involved in a slew of off-field incidents and never contributed on the field.

Defensive coordinator Dean Pees retired ahead of the season. Head coach Mike Vrabel didn't name a replacement, but outside linebackers coach Shane Bowen inherited play-calling duties. The Titans signed prized free-agent outside linebacker Jadeveon Clowney days before the season started. Clowney proved to be a disappointment, recording zero sacks before ending the season on injured reserve.

Tennessee began 2020 with five straight victories, including a Week 5 triumph over the Buffalo Bills. Positive COVID-19 tests within the Titans' head-quarters forced a modified schedule. As a result, Tennessee and Buffalo took part in the second NFL game to be played on a Tuesday since 1948.

The Titans rode superstar running back Derrick Henry all the way to the playoffs. Henry rushed for 2,027 yards on the way to NFL Offensive Player of the Year. (See page 164.) With an 11–5 record, the Titans won their first AFC South Division title since 2008.

They hosted the Baltimore Ravens in the wild-card round, setting up a rematch of the previous season's divisional round. The Ravens exacted revenge. The Titans blew a 10–0 lead and were defeated, 20–13. Given the success of the regular season, it felt like a missed opportunity for another memorable playoff run.

Schedule

	OPPONENT	SCORE	RECORD
W	@ Denver Broncos	16–14	1–0
W	Jacksonville Jaguars	33–30	2–0
W	@ Minnesota Vikings	31–30	3–0
W	Buffalo Bills	42–16	4–0
W	Houston Texans (OT)	42–36	5–0
L	Pittsburgh Steelers	24–27	5–1
L	@ Cincinnati Bengals	20–31	5–2
W	Chicago Bears	24–17	6–2
L	Indianapolis Colts	17–34	6–3
W	@ Baltimore Ravens (OT)	30–24	7–3
W	@ Indianapolis Colts	45–26	8–3
L	Cleveland Browns	35–41	8–4
W	@ Jacksonville Jaguars	31–10	9–4
W	Detroit Lions	46–25	10–4
L	@ Green Bay Packers	14–40	10–5
W	@ Houston Texans	41–38	11–5
L	*Baltimore Ravens*	*13–20*	*0–1*

Season Leaders

CATEGORY	TOTAL	PLAYER
Passing Yards	3,819	Ryan Tannehill
Rushing Yards	2,027	Derrick Henry
Receiving Yards	1,075	A.J. Brown
Receptions	70	A.J. Brown
Interceptions	4	M. Butler, A. Hooker
Sacks	5.5	Harold Landry
Points	104	Derrick Henry

Key Additions:
Jadeveon Clowney (DE)

Starting Lineup

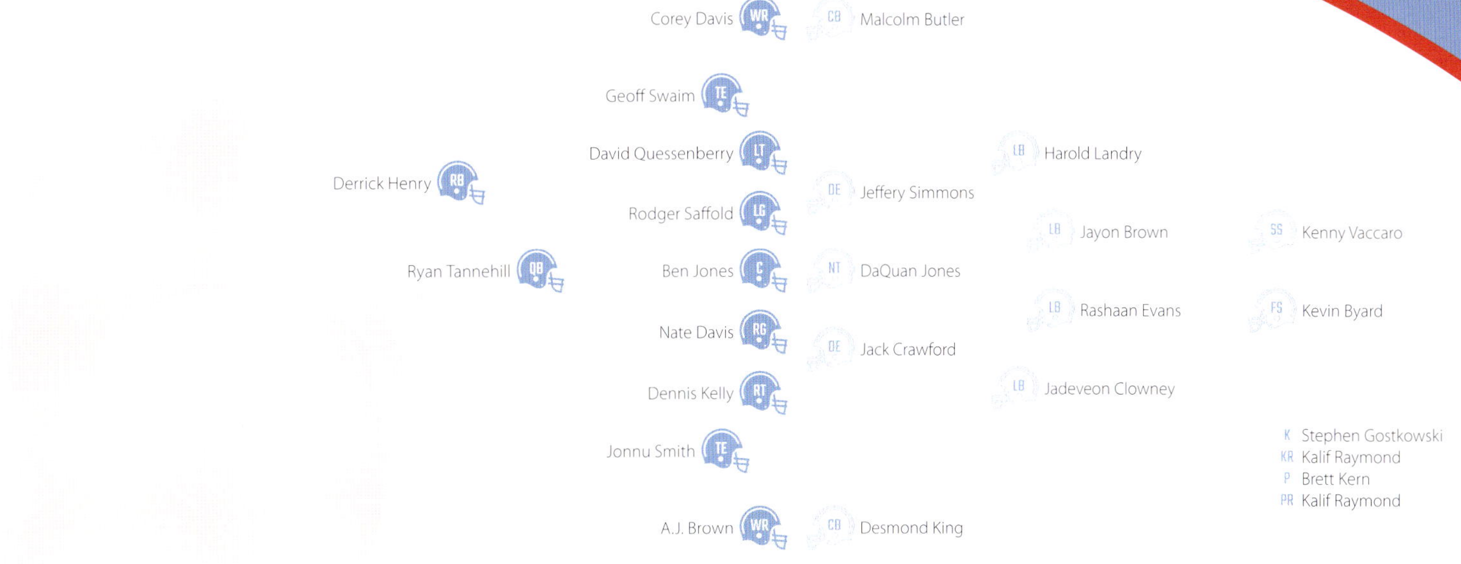

Titans Trivia

The Titans scored 491 points in 2020, the most they've scored in a season since 1961.

Pro Bowl Selections

- A.J. Brown (WR)
- Derrick Henry (RB)

Oh, Henry!

Derrick Henry cemented himself as one of the NFL's best running backs in 2019, rushing for a league-leading 1,540 yards and 16 touchdowns. He helped carry the Titans to the AFC Championship Game.

Henry elevated his game to new heights in 2020, rushing for more than 200 yards on three occasions—including a 212-yard, two-touchdown performance in a thrilling 42–36 overtime win over the Houston Texans. Henry ran for 133 yards and a touchdown against the Baltimore Ravens, including a 29-yard walk-off touchdown in overtime for a 30–24 win.

In the chase for 2,000 rushing yards, Henry entered the regular-season finale 223 yards short. The odds were against him, but he responded with a legendary performance. He set a single-game franchise record with 250 yards on the ground, bringing his season total to 2,027 yards.

He was named the NFL Offensive Player of the Year, becoming the eighth running back in league history to rush for more than 2,000 yards in a season, joining former Titans running back Chris Johnson on a very short and very elite list.

Derrick Henry led the NFL in rushing attempts four times.

22
TITANS

2021

12–5
First in AFC South

In 2021, the NFL added a 17th game to the schedule. Titans offensive coordinator Arthur Smith was hired as head coach of the Atlanta Falcons. Mike Vrabel replaced him by promoting tight ends coach Todd Downing. Shane Bowen was officially named the defensive coordinator.

Offseason departures included Malcolm Butler, Jadeveon Clowney, Corey Davis, and DaQuan Jones. Denico Autry proved to be the Titans' top free-agent pickup. Tennessee also acquired veteran wide receiver and potential hall-of-famer Julio Jones from the Falcons. However, injuries and advancing age prevented him from reaching his ceiling.

The season began in uneven fashion. The Titans started 2–2 before hitting their stride, but disaster struck in the midst of a Week 8 victory over the Indianapolis Colts: Superstar running back Derrick Henry suffered a foot injury that kept him out for the rest of the regular season. At the time of his injury, Henry was leading the league in rushing yards and touchdowns, and he was on pace for another potential 2,000-yard season.

Surprisingly, the Titans kept rolling despite the loss of Henry. In fact, Vrabel kept the Titans afloat in the face of mounting injuries. The Titans used an NFL-record 91 players throughout the course of the season. Routine lineup changes didn't prevent them from clinching the AFC's top seed with a Week 18 win over the Houston Texans. Vrabel earned Coach of the Year honors for his efforts.

The Titans claimed a first-round bye, and the road to Super Bowl LVI would have to travel through Nashville. An emotional boost was provided when Henry returned to the field for postseason play. Unfortunately, the Titans were stunned by the Cincinnati Bengals in the divisional round. Quarterback Ryan Tannehill threw three interceptions, the last of which occurred with 20 seconds left in a 16–16 game. It set up the Bengals for a 52-yard game-winning field goal.

In a season that saw the Titans defeat Super Bowl contenders like the Los Angeles Rams, Kansas City Chiefs, and Buffalo Bills, Tennessee appeared positioned for a run at Super Bowl LVI. The disappointing loss lingered.

Schedule

	OPPONENT	SCORE	RECORD
L	Arizona Cardinals	13–38	0–1
W	@ Seattle Seahawks (OT)	33–30	1–1
W	Indianapolis Colts	25–16	2–1
L	@ New York Jets (OT)	24–27	2–2
W	@ Jacksonville Jaguars	37–19	3–2
W	Buffalo Bills	34–31	4–2
W	Kansas City Chiefs	27–3	5–2
W	@ Indianapolis Colts (OT)	34–31	6–2
W	@ Los Angeles Rams	28–16	7–2
W	New Orleans Saints	23–21	8–2
L	Houston Texans	13–22	8–3
L	@ New England Patriots	13–36	8–4
W	Jacksonville Jaguars	20–0	9–4
L	@ Pittsburgh Steelers	13–19	9–5
W	San Francisco 49ers	20–17	10–5
W	Miami Dolphins	34–3	11–5
W	@ Houston Texans	28–25	12–5
L	*Cincinnati Bengals*	*16–19*	*0–1*

Season Leaders

CATEGORY	TOTAL	PLAYER
Passing Yards	3,734	Ryan Tannehill
Rushing Yards	937	Derrick Henry
Receiving Yards	869	A.J. Brown
Receptions	63	A.J. Brown
Interceptions	5	Kevin Byard
Sacks	12	Harold Landry
Points	120	Randy Bullock

Key Additions:
Denico Autry (DE), Julio Jones (WR)

Starting Lineup

Titans Trivia

The 2021 Titans won the franchise's first back-to-back division title since 1962.

Pro Bowl Selections

- Kevin Byard (S)
- Harold Landry (LB)
- Rodger Saffold (G)
- Jeffery Simmons (DT)

2022

7–10
Second in AFC South

General manager Jon Robinson traded Pro Bowl wide receiver A.J. Brown to the Philadelphia Eagles during the 2023 NFL Draft. Brown and the Titans had been involved in a contract-related standoff. It was a catastrophic move. Robinson drafted wide receiver Treylon Burks with the first-round pick acquired in the trade. Quarterback Malik Willis was selected in the third round. The Titans also added veteran receiver Robert Woods to the roster.

Undrafted punter Ryan Stonehouse won a roster spot over Brett Kern, who was released. Stonehouse proved himself to be a worthy successor, averaging a single-season NFL record of 53.1 yards per punt.

Injuries came in waves for a second straight year. Linebacker Harold Landry suffered a season-ending injury in training camp. Early in the season, left tackle Taylor Lewan tore his ACL for the second time in three years.

A five-game winning streak offered fans hope, but quarterback Ryan Tannehill injured his ankle in a Week 7 victory over the Indianapolis Colts. He returned a few weeks later.

The Titans were blown out, 35–10, by the Eagles in Week 13. Brown torched his former team, recording eight receptions for 119 yards and two touchdowns. Two days later, Robinson was fired as general manager.

Tannehill reaggrevated his ankle in Week 15 and was eventually placed on injured reserve. Willis struggled in Tannehill's place, prompting the Titans to sign veteran quarterback Joshua Dobbs.

Tennessee lost their final seven games but, surprisingly, still had a chance to win the weak AFC South going into the final game. The Titans fielded 86 players throughout 2022 as injuries plagued the team for a second straight season. A league-high 34 players were placed on injured reserve.

Schedule

	OPPONENT	SCORE	RECORD
L	New York Giants	20–21	0–1
L	@ Buffalo Bills	7–41	0–2
W	Las Vegas Raiders	24–22	1–2
W	@ Indianapolis Colts	24–17	2–2
W	@ Washington Commanders	21–17	3–2
W	Indianapolis Colts	19–10	4–2
W	@ Houston Texans	17–10	5–2
L	@ Kansas City Chiefs (OT)	17–20	5–3
W	Denver Broncos	17–10	6–3
W	@ Green Bay Packers	27–17	7–3
L	Cincinnati Bengals	16–20	7–4
L	@ Philadelphia Eagles	10–35	7–5
L	Jacksonville Jaguars	22–36	7–6
L	@ Los Angeles Chargers	14–17	7–7
L	Houston Texans	14–19	7–8
L	Dallas Cowboys	13–27	7–9
L	@ Jacksonville Jaguars	16–20	7–10

Season Leaders

CATEGORY	TOTAL	PLAYER
Passing Yards	2,536	Ryan Tannehill
Rushing Yards	1,538	Derrick Henry
Receiving Yards	527	Robert Woods
Receptions	53	Robert Woods
Interceptions	4	Kevin Byard
Sacks	8	Denico Autry
Points	79	Randy Bullock

Pro Bowl Selections

- Morgan Cox (LS)
- Derrick Henry (RB)
- Ben Jones (C)
- Jeffery Simmons (DT)

Key Additions:
Ryan Stonehouse (P)

Jeffery Simmons was Second-Team All-Pro in 2021 and 2022.

Starting Lineup

OFFENSE	POSITION
Ryan Tannehill	QB
Derrick Henry	RB
Nick Westbrook-Ikhine	WR
Robert Woods	WR
Geoff Swaim	TE
Chigoziem Okonkwo	TE
Dennis Daley	LT
Aaron Brewer	LG
Ben Jones	C
Nate Davis	RG
Nicholas Petit-Frere	RT

DEFENSE	POSITION
DeMarcus Walker	DE
Teair Tart	NT
Jeffery Simmons	DE
Bud Dupree	OLB
David Long	ILB
Dylan Cole	ILB
Bud Dupree	OLB
Roger McCreary	CB
Kristian Fulton	CB
Kevin Byard	SS
Andrew Adams	FS

SPECIAL TEAMS	POSITION
Randy Bullock	K
Hassan Haskins	KR
Ryan Stonehouse	P
C.J. Board	PR

2023

6–11
Fourth in AFC South

The Titans hired Ran Carthon as their general manager. In his first offseason, he released notable veterans Taylor Lewan, Bud Dupree, and Robert Woods. Mike Vrabel relieved offensive coordinator Todd Downing of his duties. Passing game coordinator Tim Kelly was promoted as Downing's replacement.

The Titans drafted a quarterback for the second year in a row. Carthon traded up in the second round to select Will Levis. After a long courting period, the Titans signed free-agent wide receiver DeAndre Hopkins. He surpassed expectations, recording 75 receptions and gaining more than 1,000 yards for the first time since 2020.

In Week 6, quarterback Ryan Tannehill suffered his third ankle injury in two seasons. Levis started Tennessee's next game, making his NFL debut against the Atlanta Falcons. He enjoyed a historic showing with 238 yards passing and four touchdowns, becoming just the third rookie quarterback to throw four touchdown passes in his NFL debut.

The Titans struggled to the finish line, but Levis flashed promise as a potential franchise quarterback. The Titans achieved a dramatic victory over the Miami Dolphins in Week 14, scoring two touchdowns in the final 2:30 to become the first NFL team in history to overcome a 14-point deficit in the final three minutes and claim victory in regulation.

Team owner Amy Adams Strunk surprisingly fired Vrabel at the conclusion of the season. Rumors emerged of a power struggle between Vrabel and Carthon, who had been appointed by Adams Strunk. The Titans hired former Cincinnati Bengals offensive coordinator Brian Callahan as Vrabel's successor. Callahan had a proven track record of developing quarterbacks.

Henry's contract expired, and he signed with the Baltimore Ravens in free agency. He left as the franchise's all-time rushing touchdowns leader (90) and ranks second in rushing yards (9,502). The Titans made several eye-popping acquisitions during the offseason. They signed free agent wide receiver Calvin Ridley and acquired cornerback L'Jarius Sneed via trade. The Titans now have a quarterback they believe in and are building a Super Bowl contender around him.

Schedule

	OPPONENT	SCORE	RECORD
L	@ New Orleans Saints	15–16	0–1
W	Los Angeles Chargers (OT)	27–24	1–1
L	@ Cleveland Browns	3–27	1–2
W	Cincinnati Bengals	27–3	2–2
L	@ Indianapolis Colts	16–23	2–3
L	Baltimore Ravens *(London)*	16–24	2–4
W	Atlanta Falcons	28–23	3–4
L	@ Pittsburgh Steelers	16–20	3–5
L	@ Tampa Bay Buccaneers	6–20	3–6
L	@ Jacksonville Jaguars	14–34	3–7
W	Carolina Panthers	17–10	4–7
L	Indianapolis Colts (OT)	28–31	4–8
W	@ Miami Dolphins	28–27	5–8
L	Houston Texans (OT)	16–19	5–9
L	Seattle Seahawks	17–20	5–10
L	@ Houston Texans	3–26	5–11
W	Jacksonville Jaguars	28–20	6–11

Season Leaders

CATEGORY	TOTAL	PLAYER
Passing Yards	1,808	Will Levis
Rushing Yards	1,167	Derrick Henry
Receiving Yards	1,057	DeAndre Hopkins
Receptions	75	DeAndre Hopkins
Interceptions	2	Sean Murphy-Bunting
Sacks	11.5	Denico Autry
Points	115	Nick Folk

Key Additions:
DeAndre Hopkins (WR), Will Levis (QB)

Starting Lineup

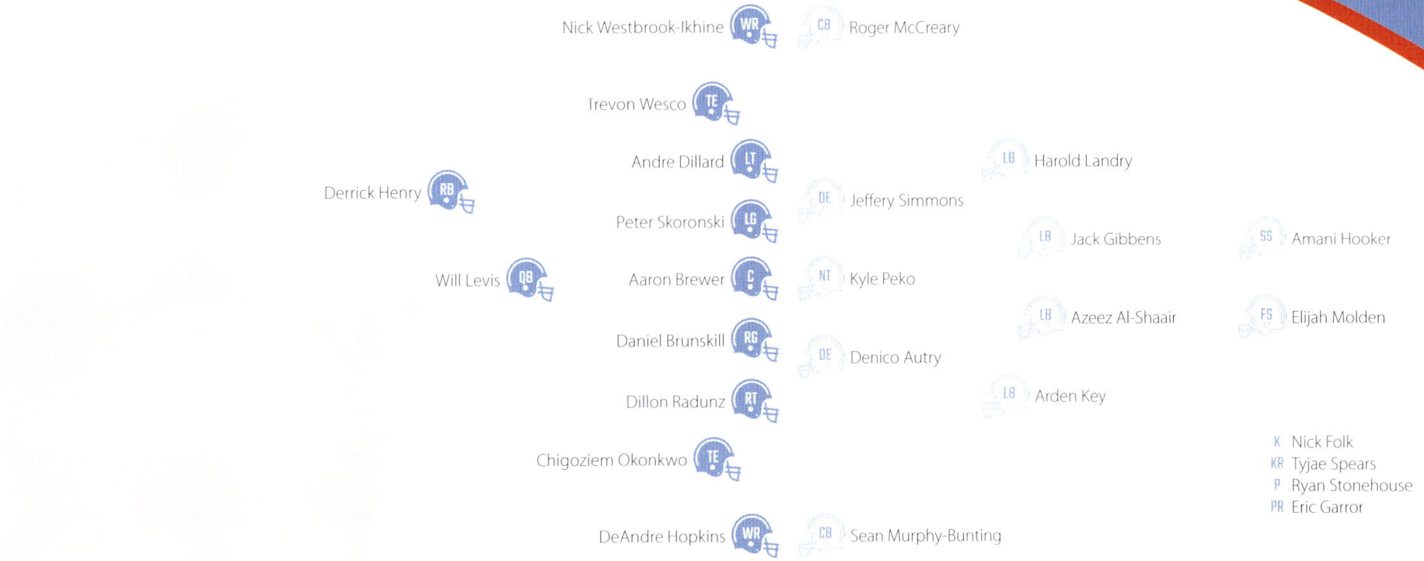

Titans Trivia

Construction for the Titans' new stadium began in 2024. It is scheduled to open in 2027.

Pro Bowl Selections

- Derrick Henry (RB)

PHOTO CREDITS

Abhishek B L/Shutterstock.com: p. 11 et. al (sword); **Felix Mizioznikov**/Shutterstock.com: p. 7 (stadium); **moondes**/Shutterstock.com: p. 11 et. al (seal background); **mostafa aboele-la**/Shutterstock.com: p. 11 et. al (warrior background); **popicon**/Shutterstock.com: p. 11 et. al (helmet icons).

The following images are copyright 2024 The Associated Press: Jeffery Simmons photograph (p. 169) by **John Amis**; Kevin Byard photograph (p. 155) by **Austin Anthony**; George Blanda photograph (p. 19), Jim Norton photograph (p. 27), Charley Hennigan photograph (p. 33), and Earl Campbell photograph (p. 55) by **Associated Press**; Craig Hentrich photograph (p. 117) and Keith Bulluck photograph (p. 137) by **Scott Boehm**; Drew Hill photograph (p. 83) by **R. Carson**; Robert Brazile photograph (p. 65) by **Richard J. Carson**; Steve McNair photograph (p. 125) by **Tim Clark**; Jurrell Casey photograph (p. 151) by **Tom DiPace**; Warren Moon photograph (p. 86) by **Mark Duncan**; Elvin Bethea photograph (p. 29), Curley Culp photograph (p. 47), and Billy Johnson photograph (p. 49) by **David Durochik**; Bud Adams photograph (p. 99) by **Mark Humphrey**; Willie Alexander photograph (p. 37) by **Rusty Kennedy**; Ken Houston photograph (p. 40), Ted Washington photograph (p. 45), and Ken Burrough photograph (p. 51) by **Ed Kolenovsky**; Brad Hopkins photograph (p. 123) by **Kirby Lee**; Ryan Tannehill photograph (p. 159) by **G. Newman Lowrance**; Haywood Jeffires photograph (p. 89), William Fuller photograph (p. 93), Kevin Dyson photograph (p. 109), and Jevon Kearse photograph (p. 115) by **Al Messerschmidt**; Gregg Bingham photograph (p. 63) by **Peter Read Miller**; Rob Bironas photograph (p. 141) and Taylor Lewan photograph (p. 153) by **Wade Payne**; Zeke Moore photograph (p. 35) by **RHS**; Derrick Henry photograph (p. 165) by **Joe Robbins**; Samari Rolle photograph (p. 113), Kyle Vanden Bosch photograph (p. 129), Albert Haynesworth photograph (p. 131), sideline photograph (p. 133), Michael Griffin photograph (p. 139), and Eddie George photograph (p. 146) by **John Russell**; Ray Childress photograph (p. 79) by **David Scarbrough**; Billy Cannon photograph (p. 15) by **David F. Smith**; offensive line photograph (p. 68), Ernest Givins photograph (p. 75), and Cris Dishman photograph (p. 95) by **Paul Spinelli**; Blaine Bishop photograph (p. 111) by **David Stluka**; Brett Kern photograph (p. 161) by **Damian Strohmeyer**; Frank Wycheck photograph (p. 105) by **Greg Trott**; Derrick Mason photograph (p. 120) by **Nick Wass**; and Dan Pastorini photograph (p. 59) by **Cliff Welch**.

COLLECT THE FAVORITE FOOTBALL TEAMS SERIES

SOURCES

Schedules and statistics found at

- Tennessee Titans Media Guide
- The Football Database (footballdb.com)
- Pro Football Reference (pro-football-reference.com)

"1980s: The Fight for Free Agency." NFL Players Association (nflpa.com). Accessed April 8, 2024.

Argabright, Brian. "News—Del Rio Legend Sidney Blanks Memorialized by Friends, Family." *The 830 Times* (830times.com). December 22, 2021.

Baca, Michael. "Titans LT Taylor Lewan (Knee) to Miss Remainder of 2022 Season." NFL (nfl.com). September 24, 2022.

Bacanskas, Julie. "DeMarco Murray Traded to Tennessee." Philadelphia Eagles (philadelphiaeagles.com). March 9 ,2016.

Benne, Jon. "Jake Locker Injury: Titans QB Reportedly Has Season-Ending Foot Injury." SB Nation (sbnation.com). November 10, 2013.

Boclair, David. "A Timeline of Isaiah Wilson's Most Notable NFL Moments." *Sports Illustrated* (si.com). March 24, 2021.

Boyd, Justin. "Taking Flak Excerpt: Pastorini Wins Power Play with Coordinator." Chron: Ultimate Texans (blog.chron.com). November 13, 2011.

Bretherton, George. "Was the Terrible Towel Incident Really So Awful?" *The New York Times* (nytimes.com). December 23, 2008.

BT Staff. "Adams Buys Back Stock from Founder's Family." Bulk Transporter (bulktransporter.com). November 8, 2022.

Byrne, Kerry J. "The 5.0 Club: Run Defense in '11 Lit up Like Hippies in '69." Cold, Hard Football Facts (coldhardfootballfacts.com). May 10, 2012.

Carroll, Charlotte. "Report: Titans Tight End Delanie Walker Expected to Miss Season with Ankle Injury." ESPN (espn.com). *Sports Illustrated* (si.com). September 10, 2018.

CBS News (cbsnews.com).

- "Vince Young Meltdown: Should Titans Let QB Go?" November 30, 2010.
- "Titans Tap Ex-Giants QB Coach as Coordinator." February 16, 2011.
- "Titans RB Chris Johnson Ends Holdout." September 1, 2011.

Chavez, Chris. "Titans Coaches Rated Vince Young Below Matt Leinart, Jay Cutler Ahead of 2006 Draft." *Sports Illustrated* (si.com). June 27, 2017.

Clayton, John. "Sprained MCL to Keep Titans' Young out of Lineup." ESPN (espn.com). September 10, 2008.

Curtis, Charles. "Remembering When Buddy Ryan Punched Fellow Coach Kevin Gilbride on the Sideline." *USA Today* (usatoday.com). June 28, 2016.

"Dallas Survives Houston Rally, Goof; Captures AFL Crown in Overtime." *Eugene Register-Guard*. December 24, 1962.

deGravelles, Charles. *Billy Cannon: A Long, Long Run*. Baton Rouge, LA: Louisiana State University Press. September 7, 2015.

Dufresne, Chris. "Rams Give up Hill, Fuller, in Bid for Everett." *Los Angeles Times* (latimes.com). September 19, 1986.

Edholm, Eric. "Titans Place QB Ryan Tannehill (Ankle) on Injured Reserve; Season Likely Over." NFL (nfl.com). December 29, 2022.

ESPN (espn.com).

- "George Dislocates Shoulder but Plays in Third." January 3, 2004.
- "Henry Suspended Four Games for Substance Abuse." September 26, 2005.
- "Arbiter: Titans Must Let McNair Work out at Facilities." May 31, 2006.
- "Pacman Faces Felony Charges in Shooting That Paralyzed Man." June 20, 2007.
- "Timeline of Trouble for Pacman Jones." January 8, 2009.
- "Titans Stun Ravens, Head to AFC Title Game with 28–12 Win." January 11, 2020.
- "Curley Culp, Hall of Fame Nose Tackle for Kansas City Chiefs, Houston Oilers, Dies at 75." November 27, 2021.

Fox, David. "Titans Owner Amy Adams Strunk Tells Fans It's Time 'to Get to Know Me.'" ESPN (espn.com). February 18, 2016.

George, Thomas. "Moon: He Wears No. 1, and He's Playing Like It." *The New York Times* (nytimes.com). October 21, 1990.

Getzenberg, Alaina. "How the Buffalo Bills Pulled off the Greatest Comeback in NFL History." ESPN (espn.com). October 18, 2021.

Glennon, John. "A Car Chase, Cheeseburgers and Everything in Between: The Titans' Quest to Sign Peyton Manning." *Sports Illustrated* (si.com). June 11, 2020.

"Gold Jacket Spotlight: Ken Houston Part of Lopsided 5-for-1 Trade." Pro Football Hall of Fame (profootballhof.com). December 12, 2021.

Goldaper, Sam. "Jets' Trade for Ex-Oiler Safety Looking Slick." *The New York Times* (nytimes.com). August 26, 1970.

Gutierrez, Paul. "Billy 'White Shoes' Johnson's Funky Chicken to Ocho Cinco's Riverdance, Celebrations Have Become the Show Within the Show." *The Sacramento Bee*. December 28, 2007.

Haltom, Rodney. "A Life of Successful Football for Jim Eddy." *Eufaula Indian Journal* (eufaulaindianjournal.com). July 12, 2023.

Heisler, Mark. "The Life and Times of the Tooz." *Los Angeles Times* (latimes.com). July 9, 1989.

Hensley, Jamison. "McNair's Case to Be Heard Today in Tenn." *The Baltimore Sun* (baltimoresun.com). May 16, 2006.

"Houston Trades Beathard." *The Victoria Advocate*. January 22, 1970.

"Injuries Don't Faze Titans." *The Washington Times* (washingtontimes.com). November 27, 2003.

"Injury Trend Hits Moon and Aikman." *Los Angeles Times* (latimes.com). December 24, 1990.

"Jags Playing for Momentum, Titans Need Win for Playoff Spot." *USA Today* (usatoday.com). December 29, 2017.

"K.S. Adams." Oklahoma Hall of Fame (oklahomahof.com). Accessed April 1, 2024.

"Kenny Britt Injury Huge Loss for Titans." *Sports Illustrated* (si.com). September 26, 2011.

Kirkpatrick, Curry. "Hallelujah. He's. Uh. Bum." *Sports Illustrated* (vault.si.com). October 27, 1980.

Klemko, Robert. "Updated: The Baffling Death of Rob Bironas." *Sports Illustrated* (si.com). October 1, 2014.

Kuharsky, Paul. "NFL Fined Titans over Ownership Structure in 2015." ESPN (espn.com). September 18, 2016.

Lam, Quang M. "Jadeveon Clowney Agrees to 1-Year Deal Worth up to $15M with Titans." NFL (nfl.com). September 6, 2020.

Lazarus, Adam. "NFL Lockout: Ranking the Fallouts from Worst Sports Labor Disputes Ever." Bleacher Report (bleacherreport.com). March 2, 2011.

Lytle, Kevin. "Tennessee Titans Rookie Ryan Stonehouse Breaks NFL Punting Record Set in 1940." *Coloradoan* (coloradoan.com). January 7, 2023.

Maule, Tex. "The Shaky New League." *Sports Illustrated* (vault.si.com). January 25, 1960.

McClain, John. Chron (chron.com).

- "Reese Steps Down as General Manager of Titans." January 5, 2007.
- "How the Oilers Left Houston and Set the Stage for the Texans." August 19, 2016.

McClain, John. "Houston Can't Escape 'The Choke' When It Comes to Buffalo." *Houston Chronicle* (houstonchronicle.com). December 30, 2019.

McManus, Tim. "Philadelphia Eagles Acquire Star WR A.J. Brown in Blockbuster Trade with Tennessee Titans." ESPN (espn.com). April 28, 2022.

Merrill, Elizabeth. "NFL Replacements Part of History." ESPN (espn.com). June 8, 2011.

"Moon and Oilers Agree to Terms." *The Spokesman-Review*. February 5, 1984.

Moon, Warren. "Helmets Are Not Weapons." *Sports Illustrated* (vault.si.com). December 7, 1992.

Moraitis, Mike. "The League-High 34 Players Titans Placed on IR in 2022." Titans Wire (titanswire.usatoday.com). January 21, 2023.

NFL (nfl.com).

- "Tragedy, Arguments Rock the Oilers." Accessed March 17, 2024.
- "Young's Mentor Is Right Next to Him, If Only He'd Reach Out." September 25, 2008.
- "Titans' Johnson: Ravens Tried to Hurt Me in '08 Playoff Game." September 14, 2011.

NFL 2001 Record & Fact Book. Workman Publishing Company: New York. March 1, 2001.

"Oilers Trade Billy Cannon to Raiders." *Pittsburgh Post-Gazette*. September 9, 1964.

Phipps-Smith, DeMario. "Jeff Fisher Had Jay Cutler as the No. 1 QB on His Draft Board." *Chicago Sun Times* (chicago.suntimes.com). November 12, 2015.

Pickman, Ben. "Mike Vrabel: Derrick Henry Will Undergo Surgery Tuesday Morning." *Sports Illustrated* (si.com). November 1, 2021.

Plaschke, Bill. "Fisher Is Named New Oiler Coach: Jack Pardee Is Fired as Houston, 1–9, Cleans House." *Los Angeles Times* (latimes.com). November 15, 1994.

Polian, Bill. "How and Why the NFL Practice Squad Works." 33rd Team (33rdteam.com). September 2, 2022.

Pro Football Talk (nbcsports.com).

- "Bud Adams Wants Peyton Manning in Tennessee." March 11, 2012.
- "Dolphins Reportedly Will Pay $5 Million to Ryan Tannehill." March 15, 2019.

Ralph, Dan. "Moon Indebted to Campbell for Giving Him the Chance to Play Quarterback in CFL." *The Canadian Press* (cp24.com). October 21, 2009.

Robinson, Dallas. "NFL Salary Cap History Throughout the Years." Pro Football Network (profootballnetwork.com). March 13, 2023.

Romero, Jose Miguel. "Genuine GM Parts: Titans Hire Reinfeldt." *The Seattle Times* (seattletimes.com). February 13, 2007.

"A Roundup of the Sports Information of the Week." *Sports Illustrated* (vault.si.com). May 16, 1966

Scalzo, Joe. "All Doom, No Gloom." *Canton Repository* (cantonrep.com). July 30, 2018.

Schramm, Tex. "Here's How It Happened." *Sports Illustrated* (vault.si.com). June 20, 1966.

Schwab, Frank. "Houston Oilers' Strange Lame-Duck Season Gave NFL a Blueprint in How Not to Do Relocation." Yahoo! Sports (sports.yahoo.com). February 2, 2017.

Seminara, Dave. "The Greatest Rally, or the Biggest Fade?" *The New York Times* (nytimes.com). January 1, 2013.

Shah, Diane K. "Football's Persuader Is Back. *The New York Times* (nytimes.com). March 7, 1984.

Shapiro, Leonard. "Oilers Outraged by No-Score Call." *Washington Post* (washingtonpost.com). January 7, 1980.

"Sid Blanks and Life Beyond Football." Tales from the American Football League (talesfromtheamericanfootballleague.com). Accessed April 1, 2024.

Smith, Brian T. "'Oh My God:' The Oral History of the 1993 Houston Oilers." Chron: Ultimate Texans. (blog.chron.com). December 26, 2013.

"Sports People; Oilers Sign Highsmith." *The New York Times* (nytimes.com). October 30, 1987.

"Stabler Will Play for Saints." *The Tuscaloosa News*. August 25, 1982.

Stewart, D.L. "Willis, Robinson Gone. Pritchard Key, PB Says." *The Journal Herald*. October 25, 1972.

Suss, Nick. "What Todd Downing's DUI Arrest Video Revealed: 'Victory Beer' and Fear of Death Threats." *The Tennessean* (tennessean.com). March 27, 2023.

Swartz, Bryn. "NFL: The 25 Most Unbreakable Records in NFL History." Bleacher Report (bleacherreport.com). May 10, 2011.

Tennessee Titans (tennesseetitans.com).

- "A Look Back at the Career of Steve McNair." July 4, 2009.
- "Music City Miracle in "Top Sports Calls" List." January 24, 2013.

"Titans to Stick with Fisher." *New York Post* (nypost.com). January 7, 2011.

"Titans' Vince Young Faces Criticism, MRI." *Boston Herald* (bostonherald.com). September 9, 2008.

United Press International (upi.com).

- "The Houston Oilers Waived 10-Year Guard Ed Fisher." December 16, 1983.
- "Cowboys Trade for Alonzo Highsmith." September 3, 1990.

"Vince Young Loses Job, Throws Shoulder Pads, Titans Fall." KHOU-11 (khou.com). November 21, 2010.

Walker, James. "Referee Explains Non-Calls That Helped Ravens." ESPN (espn.com). January 10, 2009.

Walker, Teresa M. "Titans Owner: Vince Young Won't Be Back for 2011 Season." jacksonville.com (Jacksonville.com). January 5, 2011.

Wallace, William N. *The New York Times* (nytimes.com).
- "Phillips Is Discharged by Oilers after Controversy over Offense." January 1, 1981.
- "Saints Give Phillips 5-Year Pact as Coach." January 23, 1981.

West, August. "The Tennessee Titans Are Officially Eliminated from the 2011 NFL Playoffs." SB Nation: *Music City Miracles* (musiccitymiracles.com). January 1, 2012.

Wilson, Dave. "'Luv Ya Blue,' Bum and Earl too: When Houston and the Oilers Were the NFL's Perfect Match." ESPN (espn.com). March 8, 2021.

Wilson, Ryan. "Cortland Finnegan Isn't Losing Sleep over the Perception That He's a 'Dirtbag.'" CBS Sports (cbssports.com). August 15, 2016.

Wolf, Jason. *The Tennessean* (tennessean.com).
- "Amy Adams Strunk to NFL: Nothing Wrong with Titans' Ownership Structure." September 18, 2016.
- "Titans Lose Marcus Mariota, Game, Playoff Hopes." December 24, 2016.
- "How Did the Titans Go from Contract Extension to Firing Mike Mularkey?" January 15, 2018.

"Wally Lemm." Pro Football History (pro-football-history.com). Accessed April 1, 2024.

Wyatt, Jim. Tennessee Titans (tennesseetitans.com).
- "Goodell: Working to Get Titans under 'Proper Ownership Structure.'" March 25, 2015.
- "Ravens HOF Ray Lewis: Titans RB Eddie George Motivated Me." February 5, 2018.
- "Titans Promote Todd Downing to OC, Elevate Shane Bowen to DC as Mike Vrabel Sets Staff." January 29, 2021.
- "Titans Agree to Terms – and Sign – WR DeAndre Hopkins." July 24, 2023.

Zimmerman, Paul. "The Big Moon Launch." *Sports Illustrated* (vault.si.com). November 5, 1990.

ABOUT THE AUTHOR

Justin Melo grew up in Toronto, Canada. He began following the Tennessee Titans shortly after their move to Nashville. As soon as Justin began watching and following football religiously in the early 2000s, he became obsessed with all things Titans.

Justin began covering the Tennessee Titans, the NFL, and the NFL draft full-time in 2020 after six years of freelance work in football media. He has interviewed more than 1,000 football players, including several Titans greats.

Justin covers football for The Draft Network, SB Nation's *Music City Miracles,* and Nashville's Broadway Sports Media. He is the cohost of the Titans-based podcast *The Music City Audible* alongside Justin Graver. He lives in Toronto with his partner, Anna, and their cat, Phoebe.